Deconstructing
the NYSTCE

Deconstructing the NYSTCE

Written and Compiled by
Bridgette Gubernatis

Additional editing and research by
Caitlyn Garcia

To order additional copies of this book, contact:
Xlibris Corporation
1-888-795-4274
www.Xlibris.com
Orders@Xlibris.com
85722

Contents

Acknowledgements

This book would not be possible without the support of so many people. Many thanks to the students I have had over the years who have taught me much more than I have ever taught them. Teaching educators is one of the things in my life of which I am most proud.

Loretto Gubernatis, my mother, has been a source of guidance and encouragement since I was born. Her book The Twelve Step Program to Writing Your Own Book was invaluable to me as I worked on putting all the strategies together in this book. I highly recommend it as a resource for writers.

Other thanks go out to the teachers I have had in my life who have inspired a love of learning in me, especially Ms. Lizz Kolodny, and Ms. Barbara Shekore, that flame, once lit, never dies.

I'd also like to thank Julie Schwartzman for her optimism and professionalism. She is a constant inspiration to me. And I'd like to thank Linda Cahill for being the kind of person who cares about making a difference in the world. Thank you for believing in my vision and giving me support in ways that I can never repay. Thank you ladies so much. I couldn't have done it without you. And also thank you for the countless hours of typing and research to Caitlyn Garcia.

Thank you to the Department of Education for continuing to inspire teachers and encouraging new opportunities for learning.

Forward

WHY IS THIS BOOK DIFFERENT?

Hello Teacher,

I thought it was important to tell you why this book is different from other test prep books. To begin it was written and compiled by a teacher who only teaches Test Prep. My name is Bridgette Gubernatis and I have been teaching NYSTCE test prep for the last four years.

Every month I've worked with teachers who are trying to pass the exam. Many of my students are teachers who have failed the exam multiple times. For the last three years the Brooklyn Education Center has had a guarantee on our test prep courses. That means that if a teacher takes our course and fails, they can retake the course for free. Because of this I've had the opportunity to see what kind of mistakes teachers have made when taking the exam. I've also been able to put together a list of terminologies that are typically on the exam. Most other test prep guides don't have the proper wording for the kinds of questions that are actually on the exam.

It is important for you as a test taker to keep a particular frame of mind when you are taking these exams. Our test prep guide focuses on strategy. Many times I've had teachers come to me who have tried to study all different kinds of information for the exam. Then they go take the exam and feel that they have wasted their time because nothing they have studied is on the exam. The key to passing the exam is to teach you what you need to know and the strategy necessary.

This book is one of the most recently compiled NYSTCE test prep books on the market. So you are going to get the most relevant and up to date information possible. I have also put together three tests in one book so that you can use this book for several different exams. I know that this book will help you in ways that other books have failed.

The other difference with this book is that you can register to take a class at the Brooklyn Education Center in downtown Brooklyn if you need more support. Do not walk in to the office to take a class; we only use the classroom there in the evening. But for more information you can visit us on the web at: www.brooklynedu.org

In the next chapter I am going to share the experiences of some of my students. You will realize you are not alone in the difficulties you may have had passing the exam.

Sincerely

B.G.

Introduction

WHY DO I KEEP FAILING?

True Stories

Over the years it seems that the test prep students I meet fall into two different categories. Some of my students have never taken a NYSTCE exam and decide to be proactive and prepare. But most of my students are desperate because they keep failing over and over again and they don't know why.

I have even suspected that teachers are failed on purpose. It doesn't seem to make any sense. Usually when I get a phone call from a prospective teacher, it is on the day the test scores have come out. The tension in the teacher's voice is clear over the phone. The teacher has failed, sometimes by only 1 or 2 points. These teachers are stressed out because they have no idea what they are doing wrong.

When you think about it, the format of the test is really unfair. You never get the test back so you don't know which questions you answered correctly and which answers were wrong. On top of this, the results are given back once the exam registration is in the "late fee window" which means teachers have to pay an additional $70 or so for emergency registration, in order to sign up for the next exam. Teachers are disappointed, exhausted and frustrated. It can be very expensive to continually have to re-take the test over and over again.

Some of my teachers are ashamed. This bothers me the most. The teacher's husband or parents or friends are saying "What is wrong with you, why can't you pass the exam?" And teachers are embarrassed and feel guilty. Teachers are also afraid. I have had students who have lost their jobs, even teachers who have almost lost their homes because they have lost their jobs.

The teachers who seem to have the biggest difficulties are the SEIT teachers and/or teachers who have been teaching a long time. When a long time teacher loses their job because they can't pass the exam, often the school will allow the teacher to stay at the job as a "substitute." This means that the teacher is basically doing the same job but for much less pay. Additionally they have lost their benefits. It is an unfair situation. But teachers do it because they are afraid they will never get their old job back. They focus on taking the test again and again and the pressure mounts and mounts.

SEIT teachers (Special Education Itinerate Teachers) have a very difficult time with the loss of wages, the separation from students that they have worked closely with over years and the frustration of having to take a massive pay cut and be kept away from doing the job they love. SEIT teachers have often spent years getting specialized degrees only to find they are stuck because of certification requirements and the exam.

The most frustrating part of the whole thing is that nothing that you see on the exam ever seems to come up in the real life situations of teaching. Most of the test takers, including myself, have said "What the heck does this have to do with teaching? I don't use any of this in my job."

This is a very good question. But it is also the key to changing the mindset you use when taking the exam. **It is precisely because you are taking the exam by trying to answer the questions based on what you do in the classroom, that you are failing the exam**. The example I use to explain this to my students is a driver's license exam. This is the equivalent of the type of test you are taking. It is the secret to passing the exam.

The NYSCTE is like taking a Driver's License Test?

Yes! It is important to think about what happens when you take a drivers license test. When do you take a driver's license test? You take it before you can start driving. The test is not compiled of questions testing your life-long experience as a driver. It is just testing you on the basics and the rules of driving. By the time many teachers are ready to take the NYSTCE they have completed a Master's degree or worse they have already started teaching in the classroom. Teachers are not necessarily taught the DOE rules when attending college. Because these tests are so important for a teacher in his or her path to certification, the teacher will treat the test as a sophisticated exam based on the education they have received in college. This is the wrong idea. The NYSTCE is **not** that kind of exam.

I usually explain it to my students by using a driver's test as an example:

Q: *What do you do in real life when you are driving and the light turns yellow?*

A: *You slow down or prepare to come to a stop.*

Q: *That is what you are supposed to do, but is it what you really do in real life?*

A: *(Laughs!) Actually no, in real life I'd probably speed up because I don't want to get stuck behind the red light.*

Q: *So you actually do the opposite in real life of what you'd answer on the exam?*

A: *Yeah that's true!*

Q: *Why did you answer it the other way?*

A: *Because I know that is the answer they are looking for.*

Q: *So you didn't really think about it too much.*

A: *No, I just knew that was the answer.*

Think about this. Most people when they drive on the road will break some of the rules. We cross a solid yellow line; we don't come to a complete stop at a stop sign; we speed up when the light turns yellow; we cut people off and we don't always signal when turning. This is our real life experience when driving. Yet we know not to put any of these answers down to the questions on the exam.

The teaching exams have the same strategy. It's the same type of exam: *a license exam*. This is a certification exam needed to get your license, not a college exam. Part of the problem is that most schools do not follow the rules according to the DOE. Even if your school does, most of us went to schools and the schools we went to didn't follow the rules. So we've been immersed in the incorrect system where no one follows the rules.

What is worse is that when you go to college, they don't teach you the rules. Many students who attend colleges in New York mistakenly think that the college is preparing them to teach in New York. This is absolutely false. The degrees you are getting in education are covering a broad spectrum. They are not designed in compliance with DOE standards. Many of the theories and instructional styles you learn in college are not used in the system used by New York. The system that is used is called The Constructivist Approach and it has very specific ideas.

This book is going to teach you the rules. As you learn the rules many of you will be shocked to find out that many of the things you are doing in the classroom are against DOE policy. I very often have students in my class completely stunned by this realization.

The Format of the Book:

The format of the book will be broken down in different categories. It is very important for you to read the section on the Constructivist Approach and Trap Words to Avoid. **These sections will cover the rules in detail.** The strategies used in these sections will help with the ATS-W, CST Multi Subject and the CST Students with Disabilities exams. Each test will have an explanation of strategy for the multiple-choice and also the essay. There will be practice essays and examples for each essay. I will try not to put too much information in the book so that it will be easier to read. However I will recommend resources for more information on topics with which you might not be as familiar. The purpose of this book is to be a strategy guide. When it comes to the LAST and the CST Multi, I will teach strategy but you will also have to study history, grammar and math. I recommend using online practice tests to help prepare.

To help simplify this, I have created a data base on our website at www. brooklynedu.org. You can go to the website and sign up (for a $10 fee) in order access all the materials and websites I have compiled as sources. The fee helps to offset the cost of running the website. But if you don't want to pay you can just look them up yourself online. I will provide links at the end of the book. Let's get started!

Chapter I

WHAT IS A TEACHER ACCORDING TO THE DOE?

*

Two ways of Visualizing the Teacher:

Teacher as Swim Coach

According to the constructivist approach, teaching is more like coaching. I encourage my students to think of "teacher as swim coach" when preparing for the NYSTCE. What is the difference between how we think of a teacher compared to the way we think of a swim coach? A teacher is generally thought of someone who is doing the work in the classroom. The teacher is teaching.

Many teachers have the habit of visualizing themselves standing in front of the students "teaching." In this concept teachers are the ones who are doing the action in the classroom. *This is wrong.*

This is not how the constructivist approach works. Teachers are not "teaching;" students are "learning." The action happening in the classroom is "students learning." *A teacher is not teaching.* A teacher is "facilitating learning." You have to flip it in your head or you will get many questions wrong on the exam. This is the first rule of the DOE. The teacher is a facilitator of learning. The students are learning. Thus everything should be student centered. Teacher centered is wrong.

If you think of a swim coach the difference becomes easier to see. A swim coach might at times demonstrate a style or technique in swimming. But usually the swim coach isn't going to dive into the pool and demonstrate it for the students himself. Rather he will use other students at a higher skill level to demonstrate for the students. This is presented as a goal for the novice swimmers. In addition, timing and competition in swimming begins and is built upon a swimmer improving his skill set, paying attention to his strengths and weaknesses and trying to achieve a goal (usually in skill and speed.) The student, as he develops his skills, *doesn't compete against other students*. Instead he competes against himself.

A swim coach's job is basically to **observe** the swimmer. Picture a swim coach walking along the edge of the pool watching the swimmer as he goes down the lane. Then as the swimmer gets out of the pool the coach gives him **immediate and specific feedback.** *"You held your breath instead of breathing, you are lifting your head out of the water, your arm is too far away from your body, you forgot to kick consistently,"* etc. In this way the swim coach acts as a **guide** to the swimmer. The swim coach is the **observer, evaluator and giver of feedback.** But the action is happening in the pool, not in the teaching.

As teachers begin to work in the Education field, they are often bogged down by curriculum requirements, paperwork and the reality of overcrowded classrooms. In reality teaching becomes about behavior management and test scores. But the NYSTCE is not about the reality of teaching. It is about the constructivist approach to learning. The goal of a teacher is to move the student through the stages of **cognitive development** to become a self sufficient learner who, in time, begins to **self evaluate** and take **ownership** in learning.

Think of a professional swimmer like Michael Phelps. You can imagine that Michael Phelps at his skill level no longer needs his coach to walk along side of the pool observing and giving that kind of feedback. Indeed Michael Phelps probably gets out of the pool and goes to the coach and critiques his own performance asking for support from the coach on self imposed goals. For example *"Hey coach how can I improve my speed, I feel like I am lagging when I get to the end of the pool right before the flip-turn."*

This is the mark of **meta-cognition** and **self directed learning** and it is the goal of educators in the classroom as well. *The importance of self directed learning and ownership in learning cannot be underestimated in the classroom.* This is especially important in understanding how to build curriculum with modifications for learning styles, diversity and students with disabilities.

Think of a swimmer on a team. The team creates a sense of community, belonging and motivation to other students. Swimmers on a swim team are generally not separated by ability. Even though some swimmers may be amazing, an afterschool swim team is generally made up of **mixed ability** kids. How can a swim coach work with the team? Would it be fair to only pull out the good swimmers? No. The coach must learn to work with all different kinds of abilities and learning styles within reason. The commitment and the motivation of the swimmers is very important. If a swimmer doesn't want to learn it is the coach's job to motivate the student.

These skills are what the NYSTCE is testing on. The questions about teaching will reflect this understanding. You must answer the questions with this kind of thinking in mind.

Teacher as Nurse:

Another way I encourage my teachers to visualize their role in the classroom is by thinking about the relationship between a doctor and a nurse. For many educators there is a perception that the General Education teacher is the one who directs the learning in the classroom and uses the Special Educator as a support team player. This is not how the DOE views a Special Educator. The Special Educator is the one who directs the IEP for the student using feedback from the other members of the IEP team. A General Educator is more like a Nurse working with a Doctor.

Think of a Nurse in a hospital. A patient comes into her ward with a specific care plan attached that has been approved of by the doctor. The nurse's job is to follow the plan, observe progress and to report back any problems to the doctor. Perhaps a doctor prescribed a certain pain medication to the patient. The nurse dispenses the medication with the doctor's approval. But say the pain medication is not working as well as expected. Can the nurse change the medication? Some nurses can, if they are qualified, but usually a nurse needs permission from the doctor to make any adjustments to the care plan. A nurse could find herself in trouble if she changes the medication without permission from the doctor.

This is very similar to how a General Educator works with an IEP and the Special Educator Teacher. The GE would observe progress and how the IEP is working. If the GE sees a problem she needs to document it and report it to the SE and the IEP team immediately.

Expectations of the Teacher:

A teacher is expected to always reflect on their own practices and try to improve. If the student isn't learning properly it is the teacher's responsibility to try to use a different approach. Teachers are considered professional educators. Therefore it is important that a teacher be confident in their choices but willing to also make adjustments and accommodations if the learning is not proceeding as expected. Teachers must be willing to communicate, cooperate and self evaluate. Words a teacher should use would include: Honor, Foster an appreciation of, Support, Help, Encourage, and Guide.

Teachers are expected to "Engage Schema." This means it is the teachers job to get to know her students and help create a learning strategy that takes into consideration the students culture, background, learning style and strengths and weaknesses.

Teachers in the DOE system are operating "In loco parentis." (No this doesn't mean "the parents are crazy!") In Loco Parentis means "In Place of the Parents." This is a legal obligation that means that the teacher and the school system take on a responsibility for the well being of a child in place of the parent.

The Online Legal Dictionary defines it this way:

(source: http://legal-dictionary.thefreedictionary.com/In+loco+parentis)

In loco parentis is a legal doctrine describing a relationship similar to that of a parent to a child. It refers to an individual who assumes parental status and responsibilities for another individual, usually a young person, without formally adopting that person. For example, legal guardians are said to stand in loco parentis with respect to their wards, creating a relationship that has special implications for insurance and Workers' Compensation law.

*By far the most common usage of in loco parentis relates to **teachers and students**. For hundreds of years, the English common-law concept shaped the rights and responsibilities of public school teachers: until the late nineteenth century, their legal authority over students was as broad as that of parents. Changes in U.S. education, concurrent with a broader reading by courts of the rights of students, began bringing the concept into disrepute by the 1960s. Cultural changes, however, brought a resurgence of the doctrine in the twenty-first century.*

It is important for teachers to remember that this is a legal obligation and not a personal one. A teacher must never overstep these bounds. For example a teacher should never concern themselves with "peer friendships" only "peer relationships." Peer friendships are personal but peer relationships are professional. This is an important distinction. The slightest difference in connotation on the exam is what creates a right and wrong answer.

Terminology is very important:

As you may have noticed, certain words are bolded in the preceding information. You will see these words throughout the study guide. These words are the terminologies that are used by the DOE in the constructivist approach. It is important that you familiarize yourself with these words and use them in your essays. You will also look for these words in the answers on the multiple-choice section of the exam.

Chapter 2

WORDS TO LOOK FOR:

Ownership
Self Directed Learning
Self Evaluation
Prior Knowledge
Self Advocacy
Immediate and
Specific Feedback
Modify,   modification,
Cooperation
Accommodations
Communication
Conference
Metacognition: *(this means self awareness in thinking about how you learn)*
Metacognitive strategies

Alternatives
Options
Limited and Meaningful Choices
Goals
Collaboration
Mixed ability groups
Different perspectives
Learning styles
Peer relationships

Discussion
Read and discuss
Support
Apply, application, apply to real life
Hands on
Active learning
Working in groups
(always mixed abilities)
Inclusive
Diverse
Honor
Students as Knowers
Rehearsal *(this is the opposite of memorize because it is considered active learning)*

Self evaluation of the approach of the teacher.

Working with others in the school community.

Resources   *(caregivers,   family, community, school personnel)*

These words will be explained as we continue through the prep guide. However it is important to also know the trap words to avoid.

Trap Words to Avoid: WRONG

Separate

Isolate

Make a special assignment

Have a co teacher work separately

Special seating arrangements

Pair, partner, buddy up

Group according to academic ability

Peer friendships

Memorize

Commit to memory

Recite

Rote Learning

Fill out a handout or worksheet

Read a book, hand out etc. (read should be followed by discuss)

Lecture

Teacher assigned

Teacher chosen

Teacher centered

Assign

"takes too much time'

"try harder"

Change (the opposite of modify and accommodations)

Ignore

Argue

Refuse

General and inclusive (the opposite of immediate and specific)

Give in

Give up

Acquiesce

Compliance (when it refers to a child)

"so as not to embarrass"

Whenever you see these words it is the wrong answer! They will sometimes be in the question and that is OK. In the answer they are wrong.

It is very important for you to memorize these terms. As we continue through the prep book I will explain why these terms are trap words to avoid. It is vital that you understand not just the word but the reason why it is wrong. This will help you quickly eliminate the wrong answers.

But first we need to examine the Constructivist Approach. Once this is understood then it will be easier to explain the Trap Words.

Chapter 3

THE CONSTRUCTIVIST APPROACH TO EDUCATION:

There are two very important names that are connected to the idea of the Constructivist Approach: Piaget and Bloom. You may remember these names from your classes on educational theory.

A general understanding of the Constructivist Approach can be found on the **Teachnology Online Resource Website**: I have quoted it below. This site is a great site for teachers. Please visit it.

(Source: http://www.teachnology.com/currenttrends/constructivism/)

Constructivism Learning Theory

Constructivism learning theory is a philosophy which enhances students' logical and conceptual growth. The underlying concept within the constructivism learning theory is the role which experiences-or connections with the adjoining atmosphere-play in student education.

The constructivism learning theory argues that people produce knowledge and form meaning based upon their experiences. Two of the key concepts within the constructivism learning theory which create the construction of an individual's new knowledge are accommodation and assimilation. Assimilating causes an individual to incorporate new experiences into the old experiences.

This causes the individual to develop new outlooks, rethink what were once misunderstandings, and evaluate what is important, ultimately altering their perceptions. Accommodation, on the other hand, is reframing the world and new experiences into the mental capacity already present. Individuals conceive a particular fashion in which the world operates. When things do not operate within that context, they must accommodate and reframing the expectations with the outcomes.

The role of teachers is very important within the constructivism learning theory. Instead of giving a lecture the teachers in this theory function as facilitators whose role is to aid the student when it comes to their own understanding. This takes away focus from the teacher and lecture and puts it upon the student and their learning. The resources and lesson plans that must be initiated for this learning theory take a very different approach toward traditional learning as well. Instead of telling, the teacher must begin asking. Instead of answering questions that only align with their curriculum, the facilitator in this case must make it so that the student comes to the conclusions on their own instead of being told. Also, teachers are continually in conversation with the students, creating the learning experience that is open to new directions depending upon the needs of the student as the learning progresses. Teachers following Piaget's theory of constructivism must challenge the student by making them effective critical thinkers and not being merely a "teacher" but also a mentor, a consultant, and a coach.

This sounds familiar doesn't it? That is because the terminology is similar to the beginning description of a teacher. As you can see the terminology is very important.

The Constructivist Approach Simplified:

The constructivist approach is based on the idea of guiding students in their learning. Instead of just learning information for a test, students are encouraged to embrace learning for life. It is important for students to take ownership in the learning and to build meaning as they learn. Classroom instruction should create an environment of "hands on" active learning. Students are respected as "knowers." Instead of treating a student like a "blank slate," educators treat students as if they come into the classroom with **prior knowledge** and an innate ability to learn.

(Any time a teacher begins a lesson she should encourage the students to use their prior knowledge.)

Students are encouraged to work with others to contribute to the learning process. Collaborative learning, also known as Cooperative Grouping, is used as an important foundation in the learning approach. Students work with others of different abilities to learn and share their perspectives. Students rely on the teacher for guidance and feedback. Students are encouraged to continually self reflect throughout the learning process.

This sounds like a very flexible and positive approach to education. However it is also important to remember that Evaluation and Assessment are also part of the learning process. Teachers must also know how to properly assess students in order to test to see if learning is proceeding as expected. There is a specific path that learners must travel through learning and assessment in order to master areas of education. These stages are based on the Theory of Cognitive Development.

Bloom's Taxonomy:

Taxonomy simply means categories. Bloom basically broke learning down into different categories or stages through which students pass as they are learning. The stages are as follows:

(source: http://www.nwlink.com/~donclark/hrd/bloom.html)

Knowledge: Recall data or information.

- **Examples:** Recite a policy. Quote prices from memory to a customer. Knows the safety rules.

- **Key Words:** defines, describes, identifies, knows, labels, lists, matches, names, outlines, recalls, recognizes, reproduces, selects, states.

Comprehension: Understand the meaning, translation, interpolation, and interpretation of instructions and problems. State a problem in one's own words.

- ***Examples****:* Rewrites the principles of test writing. Explain in one's own words the steps for performing a complex task. Translates an equation into a computer spreadsheet.

- ***Key Words****:* comprehends, converts, defends, distinguishes, estimates, explains, extends, generalizes, gives an example, infers, interprets, paraphrases, predicts, rewrites, summarizes, translates.

Application: Use a concept in a new situation or unprompted use of an abstraction. Applies what was learned in the classroom into novel situations in the work place.

- ***Examples****:* Use a manual to calculate an employee's vacation time. Apply laws of statistics to evaluate the reliability of a written test.

- ***Key Words****:* applies, changes, computes, constructs, demonstrates, discovers, manipulates, modifies, operates, predicts, prepares, produces, relates, shows, solves, uses.

Analysis: Separates material or concepts into component parts so that its organizational structure may be understood. Distinguishes between facts and inferences.

- ***Examples****:* Troubleshoot a piece of equipment by using logical deduction. Recognize logical fallacies in reasoning. Gathers information from a department and selects the required tasks for training.

- ***Key Words****:* analyzes, breaks down, compares, contrasts, diagrams, deconstructs, differentiates, discriminates, distinguishes, identifies, illustrates, infers, outlines, relates, selects, separates.

Synthesis: Builds a structure or pattern from diverse elements. Put parts together to form a whole, with emphasis on creating a new meaning or structure.

- • ***Examples***: Write a company operations or process manual. Design a machine to perform a specific task. Integrates training from several sources to solve a problem. Revises and process to improve the outcome.

- • ***Key Words***: categorizes, combines, compiles, composes, creates, devises, designs, explains, generates, modifies, organizes, plans, rearranges, reconstructs, relates, reorganizes, revises, rewrites, summarizes, tells, writes.

Evaluation: Make judgments about the value of ideas or materials.

- • ***Examples***: Select the most effective solution. Hire the most qualified candidate. Explain and justify a new budget.

- • ***Key Words***: appraises, compares, concludes, contrasts, criticizes, critiques, defends, describes, discriminates, evaluates, explains, interprets, justifies, relates, summarizes, supports.

I use the following mnemonic device to help students remember the order of the stages:

Kick Charlie's Ass And Slap Evelyn

Just remember "And" and "Analysis" both start with "An."

It is very important for you to understand these stages of learning. The key words above can be used when reading NYSTCE questions to help you accurately understand the goal of the question. We can simplify the stages by comparing them to riding a bike.

Bloom's Taxonomy is Like Riding a Bike:

Think about riding a bike. Do you know how to ride a bike? Think about how old you were when you learned how to ride a bike. Most people were younger when they learned. It has been said that once you learn how to ride a bike, you never forget. Why is this? This is because you go through all Bloom's stages of learning when you learn to ride a bike.

The first stage is Knowledge. Do you know what a bike is? Most kids will see friends riding their bikes and want to learn to do it as well. You know what a bike is. You have that knowledge.

The second stage is Comprehension. Do you understand how you are supposed to ride a bike? Do you understand how a bike works? You probably watched your friends riding and understood the basic mechanics of it. You sit on the bike, you balance, and you pedal with your feet.

Great! But how did you learn to ride the bike? Even if someone showed you—tried to walk you along while you practiced—the only way you learn how to ride a bike is by getting on the bike and doing it.

This is Application! You get on the bike. This is "hands on, active learning." This is the first stage of higher learning. This is the first stage of critical thinking. This is the most important stage for young students. Students are always encouraged to learn in an active manner. You mastered the first part of riding a bike.

Then what did you do? Most people started playing around on the bike. Maybe you rode standing up, you let go of the handle bars, or you rode the bike in circles. This is Analysis! You are taking the idea apart and playing around with it.

Next perhaps you decided to pedal really fast as you went down a hill. Zoom! But then what happened? In most cases the bike chain pops off. Then you lost control of the bike. Now what do you do? Well you try to solve the problem. Perhaps you put your sneaker down to drag to a stop, perhaps you turned the handle bars to steer the bike to a safe stop, or perhaps you just crashed somewhere that was safer than the street. This is problem solving, this is Synthesis.

Finally you got up and you dusted yourself off and you thought about what just happened. You assessed the situation and realized that you should never pedal really fast when you are going down a hill. And you never forgot it! This is Evaluation. You have gone through all of the stages. Congratulations!

This is the way teachers are expected to educate students in the Constructivist Approach. Students are encouraged to engage in all the learning stages. As students move through the different stages they become learners for life. The goal is to foster a life-long appreciation and love of learning. The most significant of these stages is Application. It is important for students to always be taught in an active way rather than a passive way. Passive learning is against the rules.

Sounds fantastic! But there's something that is important to remember. Piaget pointed out that until a student has developed in a certain stage it will not be possible for the student to go through all of Bloom's steps.

Piaget has four Stages:

- **Sensorimotor ages 0-2**

- **Preoperational ages 2-7**

- **Concrete operational ages 7-11**

- **Formal Operations ages 11-15**

For the purposes of the NYSTCE it is important to carefully distinguish between the Preoperational stage and the Concrete Operational stage. These are the two that are most often used to create questions for the multiple-choice portions of the ATS-W and the CST-Students with Disabilities.

The Preoperational Stage: This is the stage when most students begin their education. Children in this stage have a goal towards APPLICATION according to Bloom's Taxonomy. Children in this stage have limitations in what they are able to comprehend. They include the following:

- Egocentric thinking: students have difficulty understanding other perspectives. They truly believe that everyone thinks the same way they do. This is why sharing is so difficult for children in this stage. It is not a selfish behavior (not to be confused with Egotistical thinking) but rather a real blind spot as to how their peers think and feel. Students in this stage are also rigid in their thinking. Classroom teachers will encourage students to engage with other students to help develop this skill. Most preschool classrooms have students sitting with their desks grouped facing each other in order to encourage and awareness of the relationships of their peers.

- The Principle of Conservation: students don't understand that quantity is not related to physical appearance. If a student sees a pile of pennies on the table compared to a roll of pennies, they don't understand that the quantity is the same. They will probably tell you that the pile of pennies is more than a roll of pennies of the same amount. Classroom teachers will encourage the use of manipulatives in order for students to engage in hands on activities that help develop this awareness.

- Classification and Seriation: students don't understand how to independently break things down into groups. They might be able to be directed to do so, but will struggle to do it on their own. For example if you asked the student to look around the room and give you four categories of shapes in the room and the items that go in those categories, they would struggle. Students also have difficulty putting things in order of size or a common property. Classroom teachers will encourage this skill by asking children to "circle all the triangles you see in the picture" or similar activities. Classroom teachers will encourage students to use hands on manipulatives to practice grouping things.

- Reversibility: students have a lack of awareness that actions can be reversed. An example of this is being able to reverse the order of relationships between mental categories. For example if you show a student the following equations they don't see a relationship between them:

$$2 + 3 = \qquad 5{-}2 =$$

$$3 + 2 = \qquad 5{-}3 =$$

- Logic and Time: students have difficulty with logic and abstract reasoning. Time is a good way of understanding this issue. Small children are known for interrupting Mom while she is on the telephone. If the child says to Mom, "Can we go to the playground?" If Mom says "Yes, when I am finished the phone call we can go later." What happens next? Usually a few minutes go by and the child comes up and repeats the question. Children in this stage don't understand the concept of "later." They have difficulty with abstract concepts and logic. This is why the phrase "Are we there yet?" has been a source of humor in many American movies such as "Shrek" and even a movie called "Are We There Yet." Educators work throughout the day to introduce the concept of time in the classroom as a way of developing abstract thinking. But students will not be able to master this skill until they are in the Concrete Operational Stage.

The Concrete Operational Stage:

One way I encourage teachers to remember this stage is to think of the grocery store that is called **7-11.** Just remember the 7-11 is in a concrete building.

Children have begun to de-center. They recognize that others don't think and feel the same way they do. This allows them to work with others in collaborative grouping with maximum results.

Children in this stage should have a mastery of reversibility as awareness that actions can be reversed. An example of this is being able to reverse the order of relationships between mental categories. For example, a child might be able to recognize a fruit is an apple, that an apple is a fruit, and that a fruit is a food.

This stage is where students start to master critical thinking skills:

- Inductive reasoning-involves drawing conclusions from specific observations e.g.

All students can learn
Jenny is a student
Jenny can learn

• Deductive reasoning–Drawing conclusions about cause and effect–(e.g. Since this happened then this will happen)

• Decentralization–involves thinking about two or more properties of a problem at once

• Transformational thought–Comprehension of the change from one state to another

The developments in these stages move along Bloom's Taxonomy from the Application stage which is the goal of Pre Operational learning into the Analysis and Synthesis stages which are the goals of the Concrete Operational learning. It is an important distinction when you are taking the NYSTCE.

Chapter 4

THE PAW STRATEGY:

"WAIT A SECOND! None of this is on the exam?"

If you were in my classroom, right about now I'd get a student asking this question. Many of my students don't understand what any of this has to do with the multiple-choice questions. Maybe they see ONE question about Piaget but that's it. So what is going on? None of this is on the exam right? WRONG. Piaget questions are *always* on the exam. You just don't realize it. They are hidden in the grade. *What?* Yes they are hidden in the grade mentioned in the question.

Think of the essay portion of both the ATS-W and the SWD. Do you notice that they always ask you to choose the grade of the student? Why is that? I cannot tell you the number of students who have failed the essay simply because they did not pay enough attention to the grade and age of the student. And many of the questions (almost 60%) mention the grade that the teacher is teaching. Have you noticed that? Why? Because they are testing you on Piaget and you don't realize it. Students are often shocked to realize that if a grade is mentioned in the question it is the MOST IMPORTANT PART of the question. They are testing you on your understanding of Piaget's stages of development.

Think of the wording you see on the questions:

Mr Hasuki is a 3rd grade teacher who is beginning a lesson on science . . .

Mrs. Thompson is a first grade teacher who is in the middle of a lesson on fairy tales . . .

Mr. Ahtmed is a 5th grade math teacher who is assessing the students on their performance on a recent exam . . .

Does this sound familiar?

We want to use the mnemonic device PAW to help!

When you read a question always use PAW to help you accurately decode the question. **P:** Piaget Stage **A:** Area or Subject being taught **W:** Where is the teacher in the lesson plan? Let's use the above examples and PAW to decode the question. In order to determine the Piaget stage, simply add 5 to the grade of the student. (Most students begin Kindergarten when they are five years old)

Mr Hasuki is a 3rd grade teacher who is beginning a lesson on science . . .

Piaget stage (grade 3 plus 5 years is 8–the student is about 8 years old): Concrete operations, the student should have a mastery of application and be working towards analysis and synthesis (problem solving) Area: Science and Where is the teacher: at the beginning.

Decode the question: They want to know if you understand ways a science teacher would start a lesson with students in the Concrete Operational stage. This would include "Prior Knowledge and engaging their analysis and problem solving skills." This question is probably looking for an answer that has students asking questions about the topic they are about to research.

Mrs. Thompson is a first grade teacher who is in the middle of a lesson on fairy tales . . . .

Piaget stage (grade 1 plus 5 years is 6–the student is about 6 years old): Preoperational stage, the student doesn't have a mastery of understanding different perspectives and diversity. Area: Literature and Where is the teacher: in the middle of a lesson.

Decode the question: They want to know if you understand ways a literature would be encourage an appreciation of different perspectives by using a cooperative group learning project to set a foundation in this skill. This would include reading and discussing the books, rehearsal or role play and mixed ability grouping. It would also include using a diversity of fairy tales.

Mr. Ahtmed is a 5ᵗʰ grade math teacher who is assessing the students on their performance on a recent exam . . .

Piaget stage (grade 5 plus 5 years is 10–the student is about 10 years old): End of Concrete Operations, the student should have a strong foundation in critical thinking and analysis and problem solving skills. Area: Math and Where is the teacher: at the end of the lesson evaluating formal assessment.

Decode the question: They want to know if you understand the importance of assessment when helping students master their skills. They want to see if you understand the importance of immediate and specific feedback. They want to see if you understand that students at this stage of learning should be encouraged to self assess and take ownership in their learning.

It is important for you to always think PAW when you are reading the questions. Most of the time on the ATS-W and the SWD the goal of the question is obvious as soon as you decode PAW. We will get to more strategies for eliminating wrong answers later. But the single most important thing you need to do is to understand the PAW approach and be able to use it to quickly decode the question. Many of the questions on the exam have very long passages that do nothing but waste your time. As soon as you decode a PAW question you should go right to the answers to see if you can eliminate wrong answers. It doesn't always work without reading the passage. But sometimes it does.

Let's look at an example from the actual online NYSTCE Preparation Guide for the Elementary ATS-W.

(source: http://www.nystce.nesinc.com/PDFs/NY_fld090_prepguide.pdf)

As you can see, it is a very long reading passage. But we are NOT going to read the whole thing. We are just going to use PAW. We can decode the question from the very first line of the passage.

Use the excerpt below from a first-grade science lesson to answer the three questions that follow:

Ms. Lamont's first-grade class is just beginning a life science unit. (**STOP HERE! DO NOT READ THE REST OF THE EXCERPT. GO TO PAW on the Next Page.**) In an introductory lesson on the functions of skin, Ms. Lamont talks to her students about the skin of an apple. A portion of the class's discussion appears below.

Ms. Lamont: Why does an apple have skin, do you think?

Andrew: To cover it up.

Thai: To make it red.

James: No, sometimes apples are green.

Ms. Lamont: Yes, that's very good. An apple's skin can be different colors, can't it? The skin covers the apple up and gives it color. Another thing the skin does is protect it from germs and insects. Today we're going to do an experiment to see how an apple's skin protects it. What do you think will happen to this apple if we cut off some of its skin?

Kevin: It will turn brown.

Melissa: It will get mushy.

Ms. Lamont: Kevin predicts the apple will turn brown, and Melissa predicts it will get mushy. A prediction is what somebody thinks will happen. What do the rest of you think will happen? *[The other children agree with Kevin's and Melissa's predictions.]* Any other predictions? No? Okay, I'll cut some of the skin off of this apple, like this, and we'll put it on the shelf. We'll also set out an apple that hasn't been cut.

PAW: Let's decode the information:

Piaget: the students are in 1rst Grade. (1 + 5= 6) They are about 6 years old. Students are in the Pre Operational stage. They cannot think abstractly. Their goal is application. A teacher should use active learning.

Area: Science, since the students are in science the topics should include "hands on" observable lessons.

Where: The teacher is beginning the lesson. Students are treated as "knowers" when they begin a lesson. Teachers are expected to explore prior knowledge when beginning a new lesson with students.

Let's see how it works now. We will not read the rest of the passage. Instead let's look at the Questions.

Q. Which of the following strategies for promoting learning is most evident in Ms. Lamont's lesson?

A. encouraging students to reflect on inconsistencies between their current beliefs and new information

B. using students' prior knowledge as a basis for understanding new content

C. helping students relate knowledge in one content area to other domains of knowledge

D. prompting students to generate the questions that the teacher plans to address

The only answer that matches PAW is B: Using students' prior knowledge to begin a lesson. All of the other answers are too sophisticated for a student in the Pre Operational stage. And B is indeed the answer. Check it out online yourself.

Let's look at the next question:

Q. Ms. Lamont's instructional strategy is an especially good one for young children because of its:

    A.   emphasis on directly observable phenomena.

    B.   responsiveness to individual students' strengths and needs.

    C.   emphasis on the use of creative problem solving.

    D.   responsiveness to a variety of learning styles.

Let's go back to PAW. C is too sophisticated of an answer for students in the Pre Operational stage, especially at the beginning of lesson. B and D are good answers in general. But A is the only one that addresses the needs of students in the Pre Operational stage. Students in this stage cannot think abstractly and so need observable phenomena to help comprehend the lesson. And of course A is the answer.

And finally the last question:

Q. Ms. Lamont's questioning strategy in this lesson serves primarily to:

    A.   motivate students' independent exploration of ideas.

    B.   establish students' recognition of conflicting ideas that need to be resolved.

    C.   encourage students' active involvement in learning.

    D.   promote students' comprehension of information they have just encountered for the first time.

Look at the terminology in the answers. Do you see a phrase that relates to the strategy that would be used in the Pre Operational stage?

> A. exploration of ideas? No: too abstract

> B. conflicting ideas and resolution? No: this is synthesis.

> C. active involvement in learning ? Maybe: students in this stage use "active hands on learning"

> D. comprehension of information? No: this is not the style in the Pre Operational stage.

The answer has to be C. And the answer **is** C.

I want you to notice something very important. We didn't even read the whole question. We only read the first line and used PAW to decode the goal of the questions. This is one of the most effective and important strategies to use on the ATS-W, Students with Disabilities and the ELA section of the Multi-Subject exam.

It is important that you master PAW and have strong understanding of the stages according to Piaget. In addition it is important for you to remember that students in the Pre Operational stage will be geared towards APPLICATION because the later stages in Bloom's Taxonomy are too sophisticated for the students to master. Students in the Concrete Operational stage explore Analysis and Synthesis in their learning.

Trap Words to Avoid:

Separate

Isolate

Make a special assignment

Have a co teacher work separately

Memorize

Commit to memory

Recite

Rote Learning

Fill out a handout or worksheet

Read a book, hand out etc. (read should be followed by discuss)

Lecture

Teacher assigned

Teacher chosen

Teacher centered

Assign

"takes too much time'

Special seating arrangements

Pair, partner, buddy up

Group according to academic ability

Peer friendships

"try harder"

Change (the opposite of modify and accommodations)

Ignore

Ignore

Argue

Refuse

General and inclusive (the opposite of immediate and specific)

Give in

Give up

Acquiesce

Compliance (when it refers to a child)

"so as not to embarrass"

Chapter 5

"TRAP WORDS TO AVOID" EXPLAINED:

Some of the words that are trap words are wrong for the same reason. So we will deal with these trap words in groups, not necessarily in the order they are listed.

Memorize, Recite, Rote Learning, Copy from a dictionary, book or website, Write over and over in the notebook, fill out a hand out or a worksheet.

All of these words are PASSIVE according to the DOE. Many teachers are shocked that they are not allowed in the classroom because so many teachers use these strategies in the classroom every day. Many teachers uses memorization techniques to help students prepare for exams by encouraging memorization of times tables and math formulas. In addition almost every elementary school I know of assigns vocabulary homework that includes students writing new vocabulary words five times each. I understand that these rules are not followed by the schools. But these are against DOE standards. They are not in compliance with the Constructive Approach which teaches active engaged learning. Do not choose an answer with any of these words in the answer.

Assign, Assignment Tell, Teacher Chosen, Teacher Assigned, Lecture.

At the beginning of this book we talked about the expectations of a Teacher according to the DOE. These words are indicative that the teacher is focused on himself rather than the students. The Constructivist Approach means everything is Student Centered when you are engaged in learning. There will be questions that ask about teachers' liability issues, hierarchy or chain of command about rules in the school itself. But if the question is about teaching the students then any of the above words is an indication of a wrong answer.

Teachers are not supposed to give "assignments" they are supposed to give goals. What is the difference? Well according the Constructivist Approach, it is important for students to take ownership in their learning. The DOE encourages "self directed learning." If a teacher assigns and chooses everything for the students then students don't have the opportunity to do this for themselves.

Separate, Isolate, Special Seat, Group according to academic ability, Ask a co-teacher to work separately.

The DOE is all about inclusion. When you see an answer with one of these words in it, usually it will have something to do with a student who is having difficulty in the classroom. This can include a student with a disability, an ELL or ESL student, or a student who is falling behind in the lesson. The question will often ask how the teacher can help the student deal with these issues. The terms above are about *exclusion*, not inclusion. They are wrong. Even though many of these things are done in the public school system, they are against the rules. You are not supposed to give a student a special seating arrangement because they are disabled. If it is worded this way it is wrong. Instead you would say "make modifications as needed to ensure the student can participate fully in class. You would never say to give the child a separate seat or arrange a special part of the room for the child.

All grouping must be mixed ability. We never ever group students according to academic ability. Many schools still do this and many colleges teach Special Educators that it is important to separate the student based on ability. However if a child is capable of being educated in the public school system then you must not separate according to ability.

You also need to understand that the General Education teacher does not have the right to ask a co-teacher to work separately with a student. This can only be done if there is an IEP in place and within the parameters of that plan. The Special Education teacher can work separately with a child but a General Education teacher cannot. And a Special Education teacher cannot ask a General Education teacher to separate this student in her classroom. If you see this in the answer on either the SWD or the ATS-W it is a **trap**.

Acquiesce, Give in, Give Up, Change, Ask a colleague what to do.

The DOE expects their teachers to be professional. They do not want irresponsible teachers in the classroom who don't understand what they are doing. Although it is important to be flexible and willing to collaborate with others, when a teacher makes a decision in the classroom the DOE expects it to be chosen wisely. It is important for a teacher not to **"abdicate authority"** in the classroom. To abdicate something means to give up the power. As a teacher your job is to engage schema, understand the strengths and weaknesses of your students, embrace diversity and different learning style and combine all these things to create a lesson plan as your facilitate the students in their learning. You are working to guide them to a goal. This is serious work.

On the test there are often questions that are about questioning a teacher's authority in the classroom. Some questions will have the administrators asking you to do something outside the scope of your job. Some questions will have a student who is being difficult in the classroom. Some questions will have a parent that is unhappy with a book or topic being discussed in the class. Some questions will ask you about the "chain of command" or protocol in the school. It is important not to choose an answer that shows you being weak, giving in, changing your mind or "acquiescing." If you do work with a colleague it should show you are on equal footing with the colleague and not depending on your co-worker to "tell you what to do." It is also important not to choose an answer that gives too much power to a student in the classroom. The students rely on the teacher to guide them. Self directed learning is not the same as a student making their own lessons or assessments.

Even if in reality you would do these things, it will not be worded this way in a correct answer. A correct answer will use words like "communicate," "cooperate," "alternatives," "choices."

"takes too much time, "so as not to embarrass," "encourage students to try harder" "ignore this behavior as unimportant" "in front of the class"

These terminologies are phrases that sound somewhat normal but they are trap words. They are wrong for different reasons so I will explain them one by one.

"takes too much time" another version of this phrase is "in order to save time." This option is usually given with an example that shows a teacher who is trying to discuss a student during a parent teacher conference or in another situation that is outside the normal time frame of the job. The DOE expects teachers to always be willing to go above and beyond to work towards the needs of the students in their classroom. Any answer that has the teacher watching the clock is wrong.

"so as not to embarrass." This phrase is usually used when discussing a student with disabilities. Many times educators make the mistake of "feeling sorry" for a student with disabilities. As a professional educator, you should not pity, feel sorry, or be embarrassed to engage with a student. You should also not worry about that child being embarrassed about their disability. I've seen this type of answer in other forms. For example on a question about a student who has a lisp or stuttering issue, the option was "don't call on the student so as not to embarrass him," or "don't ask him to repeat what he said so as not to embarrass him." As you can tell it is the wrong approach. When you say that you don't want to embarrass the student, you create the idea that he has a reason to be embarrassed. This is wrong.

"encourage students to try harder." This option usually comes up when a teacher has not been successful in facilitating the students in learning. If the student has not achieved the goal, the teacher is the one who has failed. Not the student. According to the DOE it is the teacher's responsibility to re-teach the section using different strategies if necessary. Answers that show a teacher not doing this are wrong. Answers that show a teacher blaming the students for failing are wrong.

"ignore this behavior as unimportant." This option usually comes up when a student is having behavior management issues. According to the DOE the only time a teacher can stop a student from acting out on a specific behavior is if it disrupts the learning process. A student sitting in the back of the class rolling his eyes every time you say something, might be annoying to you but as long as he is not disrupting the class, you should not intervene. If students are making noise or creating distractions then you can intervene. There is an exception to this rule; that is the "Zero Reject Policy." If a behavior is considered symptomatic of a disability then the teacher must learn to accommodate that behavior. For example if a student has a tick or Tourettes's syndrome and acts out because of it, the teacher should work around the issue. But an answer will never say "ignore this behavior as unimportant." First of all we don't ignore anything that happens. Second of all, we would not say any behavior is unimportant.

"in front of the class." A teacher should never bring a student to the front of the class for either a reprimand or to be praised. Most teachers would obviously not reprimand a student in front of the class, but they wouldn't necessarily think it was wrong to praise the student. It is. Imagine you praise little Timmy for a job well done on his Math test. He stands up in front of all his buddies and is embarrassed. Timmy could decide that he will never do that good again because he doesn't want to be brought to the front of the class for praise. This can obviously affect his learning.

Pair, Partner, Buddy Up

These words are tricky. In general they are wrong when used in an answer. Although most schools have students work in pairs as part of collaborative learning, there is a difference in the wording that is often hard to distinguish. The rule I use is this:

If it is used as a noun it is correct, e.g.:

- *Have the students work in pairs.*
- *Have the student work with a partner.*

However if it is used as a verb it is WRONG e.g.:

Pair the student with another student.

Partner the student with another student.

Why is it wrong? To decode the question you have to look to see if there is a sense that this is a permanent partnership. Collaborative learning needs to be flexible and on a rotation of sorts. In other words we don't want students to always work with the same partner. Think of it this way. Say we have Jane and Kim in the classroom. Jane does very well in math but Kim struggles. So we have a high performing student partner with a low performing student. On a temporary basis this would be a good strategy. Kim can learn from Jane. Jane can develop her skills as she helps Kim. Kim can also show Jane different ways of analyzing a problem. But think about what will realistically happen if Jane and Kim always work together as partners. Eventually Jane will dominate the pair because she has a stronger skill set. Also Kim might find herself falling into a passive role because she knows Jane is usually correct. In the end Kim will begin to rely on Jane. Jane will then fall into a role of "taking care" of Kim and the partnering will be unbalanced.

To avoid this, partners should always rotate. This is not what realistically happens in the classroom. But this is what the DOE wants. When you see questions that have partnering in the answer the DOE is usually testing you to see if you know the difference. On rare occasions I have seen this as a correct answer. And I have often seen the words Pair or Partner in a question. As I said before don't worry if you see the word in the question. But 99% of the time if it is in the answer it is WRONG.

Also **never** use it in the **essay**. I know that there are essays online that use the word partner. For example the NYSTCE Preparation Guide uses a partner for the 14 year old Autistic boy in their example online. But there is such a precise way to use it that you will probably lose points on this. I have had students in my class who wrote identical essays for the CST-SWD. We had practiced in the class and three students uses the same strategy, collaboration and age. One of the students got a 260 on the essay. The other two students got a 140. We could not figure out what they had done differently. In the end it turned out that the students with the 140 used the word partner in their essay. So just to be safe, **don't use it.**

Next we will move on to the ATS-W essay. I encourage all students preparing for the CST-SWD to read this section as well, even if you have already passed the ATS-W. It has some helpful hints. The first example we will use will discuss disabilities. So take a look.

Chapter 6

THE ATS-W ESSAY:

Now that we know some of the rules about the Constructivist approach, let's take a look at how to write the essay. There is a good resource online at the Long Island University Writing Center. This site breaks down the essay bit by bit. However they use a format that is older. Also the practice prompts are geared towards the Secondary ATS-W so keep that in mind.

In the past, when I have posted links to this site, I have found that the links don't work. I believe the pages might be cached on an old link. The easiest way to find the pages is to go to Google first, then type in "LIU ATS-W Essay" and search. It should be the first link that pops up. Once you are there you can move through the site easily.

Here are two paragraphs shown on the site that demonstrate the Wrong and Right way to write the essay.

Let's take a look:

(source: http://www2.brooklyn.liu.edu/bbut07/writingc/wc_atsw_decode.html)

GOAL:

How can I provide students who have disabilities with effective learning experiences in an inclusive regular education classroom?

Writer 1: **WRONG**

It is important that a disabled student get as much help as possible in a regular education class because he/she has a disability that makes it harder to do things that are easy for other students to do. One way that I can help such a student is by making up special homework assignments for the student tailored to his/her needs. Other ways that I could help the student can include partnering the student up with a buddy who can also help and making sure that the student has a special seat in front of the blackboard. These things would ensure that the student had the support needed to succeed in my classroom. Before the student came to my classroom, I would also teach all of the students in my class about children with disabilities. In this way, the rest of my students would empathize with the new student rather than feel alienated from him/her. This would mean that my students would feel more inclined to help the student rather than make fun of him/her.

What is wrong with this essay?

First of all the entire essay is teacher centered. Everything that is written discusses how the teacher sees the situation and what she feels about it. Additionally she uses many of the Trap Words to Avoid. Go back and read again to see how many you can find.

> ➢   Special assignments, special seat

> ➢   Partnering the student with a buddy

> ➢   Making assumptions about the disability before meeting the student. (*makes it harder to do things that are easy for other students to do.*)

> ➢   Teach, "**my** classroom" "**my** class"

> ➢   The SANTA CLAUS EFFECT!

What is the Santa Claus effect?

The Santa Claus effect is a term I use when teachers behave like mothers who have an unrealistic vision of taking their child to see Santa. We are all familiar with this idea through media and television and sometimes personal experience. Like the teacher in the essay the mother is making all sorts of plans. She gets the child dressed up in a special outfit and then heads down to see Santa Claus. She has decided that her child will love to see Santa Claus and plans to get a picture of the child on Santa's lap.

But what happens? Sometimes small children are terrified of Santa Claus. They don't want to sit on his lap and they start crying and screaming and trying to wiggle off. But Mom still tries to take the picture. She's made a plan and she is sticking to it.

What does this have to do with the essay? As we can see in the essay, the teacher picks a plan that she intends to use with the students. She makes statements about how the students are going to react. She says, "*In this way, the rest of my students would empathize with the new student rather than feel alienated from him/her. This would mean that my students would feel more inclined to help the student rather than make fun of him/her.* How does she know this? These kinds of statements are wrong on the essay. You should not write your ideas about how a student will respond to a strategy. You have no idea if it is true or not. Consider the statements below:

I plan to take the students to the Natural History Museum to see Dinosaurs. Students will enjoy this trip because children are fascinated by dinosaurs.

(Except for the child who was terrified when he saw the movie Jurassic Park. Except for the child that doesn't like large crowds and big spaces. Except for the child who hates walking.)

One of the strategies that I will use in the class is having the students work on the computer. This is a good strategy because students enjoy working on computers.

(Says who? What about the child who can't deal with the fluorescent lighting in the computer screen. What about the child who has a hard time with finger dexterity. What about the child who is stressed out about the computer because his brother always fights with him at home when he is using it.)

The justification in the above examples and the previous essay paragraph are wrong. You should not make these kinds of statements in your essay. All that it shows is that you are teacher determined to do the assignment the way you want to, not flexible and not willing to make modifications as needed. Granted in real life you would not be this way, but this is what it looks like on the essay. **The writer does not sound professional.** Because of all these errors, the essay doesn't sound like a professional DOE Educator. Instead it sounds like an unprofessional teacher who has no idea about the rules of the DOE. Let's take a look at a better example:

GOAL:

How can I provide students who have disabilities with effective learning experiences in an inclusive regular education classroom?

Writer 2:

As a second strategy, I would familiarize myself with the student's Individualized Education Plan (IEP) and use it as an important resource for planning instruction. An IEP is created especially for each child with disabilities and is the basis for all decisions made about the child's education. As a classroom teacher, I must be prepared to use IEPs as I will be one of the people responsible for implementing my student's plans. The IEP provides information and guidelines for helping a student with disabilities learn in the regular classroom. It will give me useful information about the student (e.g., reading comprehension level, learning style) and identify general strategies for adapting the student's instruction. By defining specific learning goals and objectives that are appropriate for the student, the IEP can also let me know if learning is not proceeding as expected. If the student is not achieving the goals and objectives in the IEP, it may indicate that I need to change my approach and perhaps consult other professionals for assistance.

This essay paragraph is much better. I still take issue with the teacher centered terminology in the excerpt; I would hope that the teacher is less so in the rest of the essay. However, the teacher sounds professional. The goals and objectives are based on the needs of the student. The use of the IEP is clearly understood. And most especially the teacher shows she is flexible and willing to make modifications if the plan is not working. This is what the DOE wants.

ATS-W Elementary Essay Format

Make sure you always mention the grade and the subject. You don't need to write a sophisticated sentence for this. Simply write at the top of your essay:

I am prepared to teach [grade] [subject]

Choose wisely. Make the subject easy on yourself by choosing the subject that most closely relates to the essay question. Choose the grade by thinking of Piaget's developmental stages. Elementary educators should keep in mind a distinction between the Pre-Operational Stage and the Concrete Operations Stage. I recommend choosing 1st Grade or 4th Grade for the Elementary exam. I would not recommend choosing 2nd Grade. This Grade is right on the edge of both stages and is tricky to discuss.

Discuss the Goal. The question on the essay asks you to explain WHY the goal is important. DO NOT FORGET TO DO THIS. Many teachers think they are answering that question when in reality they are simply repeating it. Let's look at an example:

Goal: Encouraging Students to take Ownership in the Learning Process.

Wrong Answer: It is very important for students to take ownership in the learning process.

The writer doesn't explain why. He simply repeats the goal and says it is important. He doesn't say why it is important.

Right Answer: It is important to encourage students to take ownership in the learning process because it fosters a sense of independence and responsibility in learning. Students who are encouraged to take ownership in learning tend to do better in subjects because they are personally invested in learning. In addition it creates an expectation in the class that facilitates learning in an active and collaborative manner. Students who learn these skills early in their education tend to be learners for life.

Please remember to think of why. The essay is not asking you to discuss a goal it is asking you to *explain why* this goal is important in a student's education. Always keep it student focused and answer why. If you get stuck, think of how this goal would help a student learn. Then explain how it helps the class to learn. Then discuss why it is important for the student's future learning.

As you continue to write your practice essays you will realize that they start to sound like you are repeating yourself. This is good. The terminologies that were listed in the beginning of this book are very helpful in guiding you towards writing the way the DOE wants. After a while it does sound extremely repetitive. Don't worry if you begin to notice this. It means you are on the right track.

Your essay should be four to five paragraphs of about six sentences each. Do no write more than this. You will not pass the essay.

I am prepared to teach GRADE and SUBJECT

- Paragraph 1: Discuss the goal. Why is it important to the student? Why is it important in the learning process? Why is it important to the class? How will it help students in the future?

- Paragraph 2: Choose a strategy. Explain the strategy in one sentence. Explain why this is a good strategy to use in the next two sentences. Explain how the strategy will support the goal in the last sentence.

- Paragraph 3: Choose another Strategy. Explain the strategy in the next three sentences. Make sure you explain a few details. Explain why this is a good strategy in the next two sentences. You can write more than 6 sentences here if you need to in order to clearly explain your strategy.

- Paragraph 4: Discuss the goal again in a sentence. Explain the expectations and goals of the strategies as it relates to the goal. Conclude.

Next we will discuss strategy. At the end of each suggested strategy I will list some of the phrases that the DOE wants you to use. You want to use phrases that are active and sound supportive of the student in the learning process. You do not want to use words that sound controlling, strict or inflexible.

Strategy:

What is a strategy? Many teachers get confused by this question. The term "strategies" sounds like an important terminology that you don't remember from your college days. A strategy is simply something you would do in the classroom. It can be very simple or very complicated. It can be something you do once or something you do throughout the school year. Below is a list of simple strategies you can use:

- **Collaborative learning/Cooperative Grouping**: Make sure you mention that it you will be using Mixed Ability groups. This is the **number one** strategy promoted by the DOE. Use the following phrases to explain WHY it is important:

  ✓ Engages the students as knowers.

  ✓ Fosters an appreciation of diversity and different perspectives.

  ✓ Encourages active learning and discussion.

  ✓ Promotes ownership and self directed learning.

- **Portfolio:** a folder that keeps track of a work or tests a student has completed over a period of time. The purpose of a portfolio is so that a student can evaluate their progress and identify his strengths and weaknesses. The teacher can also use the portfolio to guide and encourage the student in his learning.

- **Journal:** a notebook where students write feedback and ideas about topics they are learning in class. Most Journals are used as a response to reading. Students can use the journal to document their emotional and intellectual response to the reading. They can use the journal to make predictions and analyze the text. They can also use the journal to try writing in a style similar to the works and genres they might be covering in class. This is a useful tool for the students because they can track progress and use the journal for self reflection.

- **Field Trip:** a field trip is a good strategy to use because students are relating what they are learning in the classroom to real life experiences. A field trip with specific goals can help students honor different learning styles and engage in active learning. This is an excellent strategy for students in the Pre Operational Stage.

- **Online Newsletter:** For the purposes of writing the essay this is a good strategy because you can make the topic of the newsletter relate to the goal very specifically. For example if the goal is about Jobs, it can be a World of Work Newsletter. Other examples can include: Maps and Geography Newletter, Math Newsletter, Community Newsletter, Sports Newsletter, Healthy Newsletter, Poetry Newsletter etc. This is also a good strategy because it is active and hands on. It encourages the use of technology. Fosters an appreciation of different learning styles and perspectives. Encourages active involvement with the publication of the news letter. Promotes ownership and self directed learning.

More Strategies:

Anecdotal Records—Anecdotal records are a form of ongoing assessment of observations of student(s) in the classroom. These jot-notes provide the teacher with information as to how the student is processing information, collaborating with students as well as general observations on learning styles, attitudes and behavior. These records are a valuable form on ongoing assessment.

Literature Circles—Literature circles are small, temporary discussion groups who have chosen to read the same story, poem, article or book.

Peer Assessment—Assessment in which one learner, groups of learners or the whole class gives written or verbal feedback to another learner. Peers can use checklists, rubrics or give a written response to peer work.

Portfolios—A portfolio is a representative collection of an individual student's work. A student portfolio is generally composed of best work to date and a few "works in progress" that demonstrate the process. Students show their knowledge, skills and abilities in a variety of different ways that are not dependent upon traditional media such as exams and essays.

Reflective Journals—Journals can be used to allow students to reflect on their own learning. They can be open-ended or the teacher can provide guiding, reflective questions for the students to respond to. These provide insight on how the students are synthesizing their learning but it also helps the students to make connections and better understand how they learn.

Rubrics—A rubric is "a road map, telling students and teachers where to begin, where they're going, and how to get there." Dr. Kay Burke. Rubrics are scoring guides or sets of expectations used to assess student level of understanding and allow students to know the expectations and what they need to do in order to be learning at a higher level.

Self-assessment–Assessment in which a learner reflects on their own learning and evaluates specific criteria in order to assess their learning. Teachers may provide checklists, rubrics or provide open-ended questions to guide the student in their self-assessment.

Let's take a look at a sample essay:

This essay was written by a student of mine who has been in the United States from Egypt for less than a year. She received a 250 on the essay and a 250 on the ATS-W.

Prompt:

It is important for teachers to be able foster an awareness of different cultural groups in their students. Imagine that the educational goal below, formulated by a joint committee of teachers, administrators, and parents/guardians, has been established for your school.

GOALS FOR EDUCATIONAL EXCELLENCE

Goal: Students will develop an appreciation of the positive contributions of cultures from around the world. Students will explore the social, cultural and creative contributions of different countries.

Examples of Teaching Objectives:

- Students will acknowledge the richness of their language, background, and culture, as well as those of their peers.

- Students will develop mutual respect and acceptance of cultural differences through appropriate work/play experiences.

- Students will use the family and community as ongoing, important resources for extending their understanding of languages and cultures.

In an essay written for a group of New York State educators, frame your response by identifying a grade level/subject area for which you are prepared to teach, then:

1.   Explain the importance of helping students develop this goal;

2.   Describe two strategies you would use to achieve this educational goal; and

3.   Explain why the strategies you describe would be effective in achieving this educational goal.

Be sure to specify a grade level/subject area in your essay, and frame your ideas so that an educator certified at your level (i.e. elementary or secondary) will be able to understand the basis for your response.

Sample Essay Response:

I plan to teach 5th Grade Social studies

It is important to provide students with an understanding of the world in which they live and how it got that way because it fosters a sense of understanding of diversity and responsibility. Students who develop an understanding of the society in which they live develop confidence and tend to do better in subjects because they are personally invested in learning. In addition it creates an expectation in the class that facilitates learning in an active and collaborative manner. A student who understands the social world early in their education tends to be learners for life.

The first strategy I will use will be cooperative mixed ability groups. Students work collaboratively in mixed ability groups. This is a good strategy to use because it fosters an appreciation for diversity and different learning styles. It also develops communication skills and the ability to share ideas about the history the community and the whole world. This strategy will promote leadership and team building skills. It will help students to understand the social world.

The second strategy I will use will be an Online Social Studies Newsletter. This is a good strategy to use because it develops computer skills. It also promotes students as knowers. Publication is a good tool for encouraging ownership. A students will learn to self assess strengths and weaknesses in their contributions. Students will strive for excellence in this form of publication. Students will choose a piece of history or literature to examine from a list of meaningful choices about a topic to be discussed in class. By using the internet students will be exposed to the online connectedness of the world which will further develop an appreciation of diversity. This strategy will also encourage students to collect relevant information about history, sequence of events, social issues, education issue and basic human institutions.

Educators, family members and the community are important resources for students as he or she learns. It is important that students receive support in their efforts to take ownership in their learning. The goal of honoring the contributions of different cultures from around the world will be reflected in the collaboration and appreciation of the contributions of students working on an Online Social Studies Newsletter.

When you write your essay you want to use phrases like the ones below:

Fosters an appreciation of different perspectives

Encourages active engagement in learning

Honors students as knows and engages schema

Promotes an appreciation of diversity and different learning styles.

Encourages a sense of ownership and self directed learning

Encourages mastery through self analysis and evaluation

Promotes leadership and team building skills.

Facilitates hands on active learning.

There are more phrases like these in the section called Terms to Look For. You want to pepper these phrases throughout your essay as you explain why each strategy you have chosen would be a good strategy to use. Keep in mind to always write the essay from a student centered perspective. By using these terms it becomes easier to stay in that voice.

The ATS-W Secondary Education Essay Format:

Now that we have discussed the basics of the ATS-W and the Elementary Essay, the Secondary Essay actually becomes a bit easier. This essay will deal with students in the Formal Operations stage of learning. Students in this age are more similar to how you would work as a student. Think of ways that you feel honored in your learning. Think of strategies that teachers used with you in high school or college that made you feel respected and part of the education process. Usually the essay will focus on assessment, use of technology in the classroom and the importance of preparing students for their future in work or college.

Chapter 7

CST-STUDENTS WITH DISABILITIES EXAM:

To begin I'd like to talk honestly with you about my experiences with the SWD. I have no background in Special Education. Not a drop. But after many of my students began to pass the CST Multi and the other exams with high scores, several of my teachers asked me if I could help them prepare for the SWD using the same kind of deconstruction and decoding strategies. I reluctantly took on the challenge but made clear that they needed to study diagnosing the disabilities on their own. I had no idea about the rules of Special Education. I looked at the exam online and other test prep guides to get an idea and I decided to try to figure it out. I did this for about six months with mixed results. I noticed however that the students who had taken the ATS-W course with me seemed to have no problem passing the exam. In fact, those students often scored very high scores above 250.

I wasn't sure what was going on so one month I decided to go down to take the exam and see what it was like myself. I honestly expected to fail it. I sort of hoped I would because it would give me an opportunity to retake the exam again and see a different version of the test.

When I saw the test, I was shocked. What surprised me was how little the questions actually had to do with special education. I was thrown off the way I had been preparing the teachers for the exam. I realized I had been focusing on the wrong strategies. When I took the exam I spent only 40 minutes on the entire exam including the essay. I left thinking I'd come back and take it again. But, I passed. Just barely but I passed. Here are my scores:

Test: 060 STUDENTS WITH DISABILITIES
Total Score: 225
Status: Pass Minimum Passing Score: 220

Underst. & Eval. Students with Disabilities	225
Promoting Student Learning & Development	231
Working in a Collab. Prof. Environment	233
Promoting Student Learning & Development	180

(notice that I failed the essay but still passed the exam! This is important!)

It was then that I realized why my ATS-W students were passing the exams. They had sat in my class where I discussed the Constructivist Approach to Education. They knew the rules of the DOE and the trap words to avoid. They also had learned how to deconstruct a question and the role of a General Education teacher.

I want to point out here that even though most of my teachers now regularly score above 250 on the CST-SWD exam, my goal as a prep test teacher is not to get you to score high on the exam. I just want you to **pass the exam**. And so I will focus on the strategy that will get you the most points.

You probably know a lot more than I do about Special Education, I'm sure you do. My goal is not to teach you about Special Education. My goal is ONLY to get you to pass the exam.

We will discuss the basics.

To begin we need to see where we should focus our energy. Subarea 1 is the section that you as a special education teacher should know. Later in the book we will have a breakdown of the different disabilities. You should familiarize yourself with each disability. There are also links in the essay section that are great resources for understanding and evaluating students with disabilities. Use them wisely. Additionally there are specific types of questions they usually ask about disabilities. In Chapter 7 I will have a section that covers these common questions.

As you can see Subarea 2 has the highest percentage of the score. So we will begin in this section.

> ➢ Subarea I. Understanding and Evaluating Students with Disabilities worth 27% of the score

> ➢ **Subarea II. Promoting Student Learning and Development in a Collaborative Learning Community worth 42% of the score**

> ➢ Subarea III. Working in a Collaborative Professional Environment worth 21% of the score

> ➢ Subarea IV. Promoting Student Learning and Development in a Collaborative Learning Community: Constructed-Response Assignment–The Essay, worth about 10% of the score.

To properly prepare for this section you will need to know three things:

- Strategies for decoding the question

- The roles of the members of the IEP team

- What a General Education teacher is allowed to do in her classroom and what she is **not** allowed to do.

Common Problems with the CST-SWD:

As you can see above, the most important part of the exam is to understand the rules of a Collaborative Learning Community. One of the difficulties that teachers have in this section is that they are using real life experience to answer the questions. This can be a problem for several reasons.

- Most schools don't follow the DOE rules

- Many schools are underfunded and have their educators double up on responsibilities so educators don't actually know what the job entails.

- Many parents are reluctant and uncooperative with the IEP process and so corners are cut and rules are bent when they should not be.

- Most schools are overcrowded and struggle with the ability to handle the needs of students with disabilities.

It is important for you to really master the Trap Words to Avoid. It is also important for you to refresh your understanding of the role of a General Education teacher in the classroom according to the DOE. The number one problem teachers have in this section is that most public schools do not follow the protocol according to IDEA law.

First of all let's think of the role of the General Education teacher. Many teachers report the experience of working in the public school has given them the impression that the General Education teacher is in charge of the student in her class and she sort of uses the Special Education teacher as an assistant for her students. Part of the reason teachers think this way is because schools are often under-funded and Paraprofessionals often wind up doing the job of the Special Education teacher.

There is another problem as well. Say you are a General Education teacher who has been teaching for a few years. Several years in a row you have a student with a learning disability in your class. You know the system and how it is done in your school. Sometimes parents are reluctant to have a student diagnosed. So you have the student in the classroom and you don't have an IEP but you use the same strategies with this student as you do with your other kids with the IEP. You know what to do because you've done it so many times before. After a while it starts to seem like this is part of your job. **Well it isn't.**

At the beginning of this book we talked about the role of a teacher being like a Nurse and a Special Education teacher being like a doctor. Let's explore that a little bit. In a hospital a Nurse probably goes through the same thing. Imagine a Nurse who has worked on a floor for a long time. Let's call her Nurse Jane. She usually deals with older patients that have typical symptoms. Perhaps she makes her rounds each day and the doctor has given all of her patients a drug. (Let's make one up, we'll call it Pixilin) The nurse gives all of her patients Pixilin and on a regular basis some patients complain that the drug makes them nauseous. Nurse Jane knows that the doctor will change the prescription to another drug that is almost the same but doesn't cause nausea. What if Nurse Jane has a patient who complains of this after the doctor has left? She's not an RN so she doesn't have the right by law to give the patient the other drug. But she knows it's not that big of a deal so she does it anyway. She will have the doctor write the order in the morning. I'm sure this happens more than people would like to admit. But Nurse Jane knows that on an exam she should never do this or admit to doing this. Why? **Because she could lose her job.**

When you take this exam you need to follow the rules. You can't go by what you do in the classroom. Let me say this again, *you cannot go by what you do in the classroom.* The reason I passed the exam on my first try is that I have never taught in a classroom and so I have never learned any mistakes in this way. I simply answered the questions based on the rules.

Let's take a look at the responsibilities of the members of the IEP team.

Members of the Special Education Community and their Responsibilities:

Principals: The primary responsibility of a principal is administrative. The principal's job is to implement building policy procedures and control designation of facilities, equipment and resources. Just remember the principal's main focus is following protocol, watching for liability issues and managing the school team.

General Education Teacher: The most important role the GE teacher has is to **observe** the student's learning progress and monitor the success of the IEP. Her job is to give **feedback** to the student and the IEP team. GE teachers are trained in general and specific instructional areas. They work with the students on a regular basis and contribute information to referrals.

Occupational Therapist: For older students the OT will work with self care skills including vocational skills. In general most OTs, who will work with students in public schools, will focus on fine motor skills.

Paraprofessional: acts as an assistant to the Special Educator and works in the classroom with the student with disabilities. The Para works as a tutor for individual students or with small groups. Creates the materials to be used in the class with the student and also gives important feedback to both the student and the members of the IEP team.

Physical Therapist: the role of the PT is to work with students who have issues with disorders of muscles, bones, joints or nerves after the student has received a medical assessment. Usually this relates to cerebral palsy or muscular dystrophy. Students in public schools may also need assistive technologies and or adaptive equipment with which the PT will be familiar.

School Psychologist: the most important responsibility of this team member is to **administer and interpret results of the standardized tests.** He will also contribute to the assessment of the student and help create the IEP. The School Psychologist will observe the student in the classroom, provide testing and evaluation and document a case history of the student.

Social Worker: The main responsibility of the Social Worker is to provide resources and materials to the parents or caregivers of the student. He or she specializes in knowing community and school services available. In addition the SW can do intake, interview and home visits as needed.

Speech Pathologist: Works with students with speech or language disorders on an ongoing basis. Offers support and feedback to the student and his or her parents and or caregivers on an ongoing basis.

The two additional team members include the **School Nurse**, who provides information to the families about health related issues. The SN is also responsible for medications, therapeutic services and care for specific medical conditions. The **Guidance Counselor** is responsible for counseling services for the family and student. They also can create and provide group counseling services.

Essential Strategies for the CST-SWD:

➢ Remember that the student is being taught in a public school. This is a very important distinction. The CST SWD is not testing you on how to treat disabled students in a general way. They are not concerned with your knowledge of special education strategies that are outside the parameters of the DOE. The test is testing your ability to teach this student **in** the **public school system**. This means that the student **must be able** to be taught in the public school system. Do not over-think the question. Do not think of very severe disabilities. Answer the question based on the Constructivist Approach to learning.

➢ It is important to pay attention to the details that are given in each question. Since Subarea 2 is worth the highest percentage of the score you need to pay attention to **which** people are collaborating in the question. Be sure to understand the DOE responsibilities for the IEP team members in the question. **Do not answer the question based on your real life experience**. Follow the guidelines listed in the previous section.

➢ Eliminate the answers with trap words or ideas that sound like trap words. Look for active learning. Many of the questions will actually be worded in a way that directs you to either "behavior management" or "active learning" and "cooperative learning." If you are left with two answers after eliminating the obvious wrong answers, look to see if one is about behavior management. When the question is asking about collaboration, behavior management is **not** a priority. Always choose answers that reflect "active learning" or "social engagement with peers."

➤ Watch out for "pity phrases." There is no reason to feel sorry for a student with disabilities. Many answers will have phrases in them that suggest the student should be embarrassed. One of the strategies I encourage students to use, is to ask yourself if you would answer the question the same way if the student was an ethnic minority? For example would you say, "Don't draw attention to the fact that the student is Chinese, so as not to embarrass the student." Of course not. Would you say, "Have a special seating area arranged for the Mexican students." Of course not. So don't make this mistake.

➤ Self Advocacy is very important. It is important for educators to encourage students with disabilities to self advocate. Because the Constructivist Approach has a goal of Ownership and Self Directed learning, one of the most important things a teacher should focus on is encouraging the student to speak for herself and not to be shy or embarrassed about having to identify her needs.

A Personal Observation:

I'd like to take a second to share my own personal experience with you as a disabled student. I use this example in my class to demonstrate the importance of self advocacy. I am hearing impaired. I use two hearing aids but generally will only wear one because one ear is completely deaf. I didn't always wear hearing aids.

When I went to college to get my MA I had been out of school for a while and didn't realize how bad my hearing had gotten. At the time I didn't have hearing aids. When I first started going to classes I realized I couldn't hear at all. I had to try to lip read what the professor was saying and so I could never look down to take notes. I constantly watched the professor's mouth and tried to memorize everything he said. I tried moving closer to the front but that didn't help. I couldn't participate in discussions because I couldn't hear what other students were saying. It was very depressing and difficult and my grades dropped. I got Bs instead of my normal As.

Finally someone told me I needed to go to register as a disabled student. I cried my eyes out when I went down to register as a disabled student. But when I did I found out a refreshing thing. First when I went into the office the director spoke in a special way, always facing me and speaking slowly and clearly. Then she told me that as a disabled student I had the right to have a note taker paid by for by the college for all of my classes. In addition she told me that if I couldn't hear in the classroom because of the acoustics I had the right to ask for the classroom to be moved. I was happy to hear this but I never used any of the accommodations because I felt "Who me? I'm going to ask the entire class to change rooms because of me? No way!"

Back then I would try to explain to people that I couldn't hear very well. Most people didn't understand because I don't sound deaf. I speak perfectly fine because I lost my hearing later in life. And so I'd tell them I couldn't hear them and then they'd keep talking to me like I hadn't told them this at all. I would just stand there and pretend that I could hear them because I felt embarrassed about the whole situation.

It took a long time but I finally got around to my own self advocacy. I learned that I needed to stand up for myself. I learned that I needed to really make it clear to people if I had a problem hearing. I also stopped getting angry and frustrated because I felt embarrassed or isolated because I was "different."

I share this story because I really want to emphasize how important self advocacy is for young students with disabilities.

When I couldn't hear in college and my grades dropped I left college for a year. I didn't think I was going to be able to do it. If I had known then, what I know now I wouldn't have lost that year in my education. I also would have been a much more confident learner. It is extremely important to foster a sense of self advocacy in your students. Students should not feel ashamed or embarrassed to ask for the accommodations they need in order to learn. A student with a disability is usually not going to "get better." It is important to develop a confidence in their own learning style by encouraging students to speak up for themselves.

Chapter 8

SPECIAL EDUCATION CATEGORIES AND THE ISSUES MENTIONED ON THE CST-SWD:

(source: http://www.nichcy.org/Disabilities/Categories/Pages/Default.aspx)

The Special Education Categories site includes information, research, resources, and best practices on the following program areas: Deaf-Blindness, Deafness, Emotional Disturbance, Hearing Impairment, Mental Retardation, Multiple Disabilities, Orthopedic Impairment, Other Health Impairment, Specific Learning Disability, Speech/Language Impairment, Speech/Language Pathology Services, Traumatic Brain Injury, and Visual Impairment.

Autism
is a developmental disability significantly affecting verbal and nonverbal communication and social interaction, generally evident before age three, that adversely affects a child's educational performance. (A child who manifests the characteristics of autism after age 3 could be diagnosed as having autism if the other criteria of this Section are satisfied.) Other characteristics often associated with autism are engagement in repetitive activities and stereotyped movements, resistance to environmental change or change in daily routines, and unusual responses to sensory experiences.

The term does not apply if a child's educational performance is adversely affected primarily because the child has an emotional disturbance.

Cognitive Disability

means significantly sub-average general intellectual functioning, existing concurrently with deficits in adaptive behavior and manifested during the developmental period, that adversely affects a child's educational performance.

Deaf-Blindness

means concomitant hearing and visual impairments, the combination of which causes such severe communication and other developmental and educational needs that they cannot be accommodated in special education programs solely for children with deafness or children with blindness.

Deafness

means a hearing impairment that is so severe that the child is impaired in processing linguistic information through hearing, with or without amplification, that adversely affects a child's educational performance.

Emotional Disability

(includes schizophrenia but does not apply to children who are socially maladjusted, unless it is determined that they have an emotional disturbance) means a condition exhibiting one or more of the following characteristics over a long period of time and to a marked degree that adversely affects a child's educational performance:

- An inability to learn that cannot be explained by intellectual, sensory, or health factors;

- An inability to build or maintain satisfactory interpersonal relationships with peers and teachers;

- Inappropriate types of behavior or feelings under normal circumstances;

- A general pervasive mood of anxiety or unhappiness or depression; or

- A tendency to develop physical symptoms or fears associated with personal or school problems.

Hearing Impairments means an impairment in hearing, whether permanent or fluctuating, that adversely affects a child's educational performance but that is not included under the definition of deafness.

Multiple Disabilities means concomitant impairments (such as mental retardation-blindness, mental retardation-orthopedic impairment, etc.), the combination of which causes such severe educational needs that they cannot be accommodated in special education programs solely for one of the impairments. The term does not include deaf-blindness.

Orthopedic Impairment means a severe orthopedic impairment that adversely affects a child's educational performance. The term includes impairments caused by congenital anomaly (e.g., clubfoot, absence of some member, etc.), impairments caused by disease (e.g., Poliomyelitis, bone tuberculosis, etc.), and impairments from other causes (e.g., cerebral palsy, amputations, and fractures or burns that cause contractures).

- Other Health Impairment means having limited strength, vitality or alertness, including a heightened sensitivity to environmental stimuli, that results in limited alertness with respect to the educational environment that is due to chronic or acute health problems such as asthma, attention deficit disorder or attention deficit hyperactivity disorder, diabetes, epilepsy, a heart condition, hemophilia, lead poisoning, leukemia, nephritis, rheumatic fever, or sickle cell anemia; and adversely affects a child's educational performance.

Specific Learning Disabilities means a disorder in one or more of the basic psychological processes involved in understanding or in using language, spoken or written, that may manifest itself in an imperfect ability to listen, think, speak, read, write, spell, or do mathematical calculations, including such conditions as perceptual disabilities, brain injury, minimal brain dysfunction, dyslexia, and developmental aphasia. The term does not include learning problems that are primarily the result of visual, hearing or motor disabilities, of mental retardation, of emotional disturbance, or of environmental, cultural, or economic disadvantage.

Issues for each category that are often on the exam:

➢ Students taking medication for emotional disabilities often experience nausea and fatigue.

➢ ADHD medication is used for behavior to calm the student.

➢ One of the most important needs of a student with emotional disorders is a safe environment.

➢ One of the number one problems for students with disabilities in regard to employment is that they often become frustrated in high school and drop out.

➢ Students with mental retardation often have difficulty understanding the main idea of a story when a teacher reads aloud.

➢ Learning difficulties are difficult to diagnose before the age of 5.

➢ Transitions are very important in the classroom. Transition means two different things. One type of transition is for older students graduating from high school. On the exam the term usually means moving between activities. If a student demonstrates difficulty with transitions then a clear transition plan should be established.

Hearing Loss creates the greatest barrier to a student's language development.

➢ Expressive aphasia creates problems with organizing words into meaningful sentences.

➤ Many students with Hearing Loss and Cerebral Palsy will have good receptive language skills but struggle with expressive language skills.

➤ Behavior disorders can be caused by many things including biological, genetic, cognitive, social, emotional and cultural issues.

➤ Muscular Dystrophy usually begins in childhood and is a progressively degenerate disease. This means it gets worse as the child gets older.

➤ Students with Performance Anxiety will find it difficult to read aloud in class.

➤ Blind students have the most difficulty with orientation and mobility. It is important to create an environment in the classroom that addresses this need.

➤ Autism Spectrum Disorder is a range of disorders.

Chapter 9

THE STEPS FOR THE IEP UNDER IDEA:

"The term 'individualized education program' or 'IEP' means a written statement for each child with a disability that is developed, reviewed, and revised in accordance with section 614(d)." [Section 602(11)]

Who Participates in IEP Team Meetings?

1. The parents of the student

2. The student, as appropriate

3. At least one regular education teacher of the child, if the student is (or might be) participating in the general education environment.

4. At least one special education teacher or provider.

   1. A representative of the local public agency (i.e. School Principle, School Administrator) who: knowledgeable about specially designed instruction for students with disabilities, the general curriculum, the availability of local public agency resources.

5.   Someone who can interpret the instructional implications of evaluation results (i.e. School Psychologist, Special Educator Teacher, Speech and Language Pathologist, etc.) who may be another team member.

6.   Other people whom the parents or the school have chosen to invite, who have knowledge or special expertise regarding the child, including related service.

Collectively, the IEP team members should be knowledgeable about:

1.   The student, available services

2.   External and internal sources of assistance

3.   The IEP process

IDEA LAW Section 614(d)(I)(B)

Section 614(d)(3)

"(3) Development of IEP.–

"(A) In General.–In developing each child's IEP, the IEP Team, subject to subparagraph (C), shall consider –

"(i) the strengths of the child and the concerns of the parents for enhancing the education of their child; and

"(ii) the results of the initial evaluation or most recent evaluation of the child.

"(B) Consideration of Special Factors.–The IEP Team shall–

"(i) in the case of a child whose behavior impeded his or her learning or that of others, consider, when appropriate, strategies, including positive behavioral interventions, strategies, and supports to address that behavior;

"(ii) in the case of a child with limited English proficiency, consider the language needs of the child such as needs relate to the child's IEP;

"(iii) in the case of a child who is blind or visually impaired, provide for instruction Braille and the use of Braille unless the IEP Team determines, after an evaluation of the child's reading and writing skills, needs. and appropriate reading and writing media (including an evaluation of the child's future needs for instruction in Braille or the use of Braille), that instruction in Braille or the use of Braille is not appropriate for the child;

"(iv) consider the communication needs of the child, and in the case of a child who is deaf or hard of hearing, consider the child's language and communication needs, opportunities for direct communications with peers and professional personnel in the child's language and communication mode, academic level, and full range of needs, including opportunities for direct instruction in the child's language and communication mode; and

"(v) consider whether the child requires assistive technology devices and services.

"(C) *Requirement with respect to regular education teacher*–The regular education teacher of the child, as a member of the IEP Team, shall, to the extent appropriate, participate in the development of the IEP of the child, including the determination of appropriate positive behavioral interventions and strategies and the determination of supplementary aids and services, program modifications, and support for school personnel consistent with paragraph (1)(A)(iii)."

At the end of the chapter on the CST-SWD the legal breakdown of the IEP process will be given. Let's keep it simple for now:

Steps for the IEP

The steps to creating an IEP are done in a specific order. Each step is essential to creating a carefully constructed plan that is created specially for each student with disabilities.

The steps are as follows:

1. **Pre-referral:** The first step in the entire IEP is to observe the student. This is where modifications are made to the regular learning strategy to see if the student can learn with a different approach.

2. **Referral:** In this stage, if the modifications in the previous stage are ineffective, the School Psychologist will create a documentation of student history and difficulties. In addition, referrals and testing strategies will be arranged.

3. **Identification Evaluations:** In this stage the different professionals will work together to assess the needs of the student. Special focus is placed upon the individual strengths and weaknesses of the student.

4. **Eligibility**: In this stage the IEP team decides what services and accommodations will be considered for the student.

5. **Development of the IEP**: In this state the IEP team outlines the actual learning plan for the student.

6. **Implementation of the IEP**: In this stage the IEP is begun with members of the team who offer support and expertise.

7. **Evaluation and reviews:** This is a very important part of the IEP. The IDEA law requires constant assessment to see if the IEP is working. Is learning proceeding as expected? Educators should be willing to modify the plan as needed.

The CST SWD will ask you questions about the steps and the protocols that are followed in these stages. This is part of Subarea 3 which discusses Working in a Collaborative Professional Environment and is worth 21% of the score. In this section you will also be asked questions about testing and IDEA LAW. Specific questions are not asked about the dates or history of the law. Rather you are expected to understand the **procedure** and the **rules.**

Parents Rights According to IDEA LAW Include:

- Prior notice of meetings and proposed decisions;
- Reviewing student records;
- The functions of the Individualized Education Program (IEP) team;
- Assessment and Independent Evaluations;
- Parent Participation in IEP team meetings and parent consent;
- Filing formal complaints, mediation, due process hearings, and appeals;
- Interim alternative educational settings;
- Discipline;
- Parent placement of their children in private schools;
- Civil court actions;
- Development of IEPs;
- Placement decisions and least restrictive environment; and
- Specially Designed Instruction and related services.

Hint! If you see any *answer* ***on the exam that says "Explain the Rights to the Parents or Caregivers." I would generally assume that this is the correct answer. CST SWD will always have one question about the rights of the parents. Anything to do with liability would point to making sure the family or caregivers know their rights. Also be careful not to just say "Parents" because many students are not raised by their parents. If you do not acknowledge this, it can come across as discriminatory.***

Other important terms on the CST-SWD:

Criterion Referenced Tests are created with known standards. Students know what is expected of them in order to pass. The assessment of the test is non competitive. The student is being evaluated only for his or her own strengths and weaknesses.

Norm Referenced Tests are generally used with students for placement among other students. These tests are often graded with a curve or a percentile.

Least Restrictive Environment:
The simplest way to think of this part of the IDEA law is to remember that the Constructivist Approach is all about Inclusion. LRE ensures that students with disabilities are not isolated and taught separately from non-disabled students. The goal is have students learn with peers. The non-disabled peers also learn from the disabled student. It is a way of keeping the disabled student in a general education classroom as much as possible. CTT classes can be used as well. Self Contained classrooms should only be used if the disability makes it impossible for the student to remain with the general population without causing a disruption in the learning process.

Zero Reject:
The State has a legal obligation to educate all students with disabilities. The Child Find system is a requirement for the state to locate, identify and evaluate all students within the state that are eligible for education.

Non-discriminatory Identification and Evaluation:
Students should not be discriminated because of race, language, or culture. Students should not be assessed by only one form of evaluation.

Free Appropriate Public Education:
Disabled students have a right to free public education. If the student cannot be accommodated in the public school system the schools must provide alternative accommodations for learning. IEPs are covered under the FAPE principle.

Chapter 10

UNDERSTANDING THE IEP:

(source: http://www.uft.org/teaching/individualized-education-programs)

Overview

The Individualized Education Program (IEP) is the cornerstone of the special education process for each individual student. As described in the State Education Department's Guide to Quality Individualized Education Program (IEP) Development and Implementation, the IEP is a strategic planning document that should be far-reaching in its impact.

What IEPs do:

- Identify the students' unique needs and how the school will strategically address those needs;

- Identify how specially designed instruction will be provided in the context of supporting the students in the general education curriculum and in reaching the same learning standards as nondisabled students;

- Guide how the special education resources of the school need to be configured to meet the needs of students with disabilities in that school;

- Identify how students with disabilities will be prepared for adult living;

- Measure students' progress toward goals and objectives, providing schools with information to determine if they have appropriately configured and used their resources to reach the desired outcomes for students with disabilities.

To assist students in becoming involved and progressing in the general education curriculum, the IEP team must consider both the state's learning standards and the school-based instructional curriculum which should be aligned to the state's learning standards. In developing IEPs that are linked to standards, the State Education Department recommends that IEPs should:

1. Review the content as well as the expectations for how the student will learn or demonstrate knowledge and skill in the content areas.

2. Identify the strengths and challenges for the student in relation to those expectations in the present levels of performance section of the IEP.

3. Identify how a student's needs are linked to the general curriculum (e.g., a student's difficulty with visual processing may affect graphing skills required to achieve the math standards).

4. Identify the goals that the student will be expected to achieve in one year. (Standard-based goals do not mean that a student's goals and objectives in the IEP are a restatement of a standard or curriculum goal in a specific content area, but rather are a statement that reflects the necessary learning that will lead to attainment of the standard.)

5. Identify the special education services, including the adaptations, accommodations or modifications to the general

curriculum, and/or instructional environment and materials, as needed by the student to reach those standards.

Every student with a disability must have an IEP in effect by the beginning of each school year. Federal and state laws and regulations specify the information that must be documented in each student's IEP. In addition, IEPs developed for the 2011 school year and thereafter must be on a form prescribed by the Commissioner of Education. The electronic IEP in the NYC DOE's Special Education Student Information System (SESIS) is designed to meet the state requirements.

Source: State Guide to Quality Individualized Education Program (IEP) Development and Implementation, pp. 1-4

Resources

- Guide to Quality Individualized Education Program (IEP) Development and Implementation

- (This is the guide for the new state IEP.)

- State Regulations: 8 NYCRR §200.4(d)

- Creating a Quality IEP: Individualized Education Program Manual, January 2005

- Alternate Assessment Standards for Students with Severe Disabilities in New York State Learning Standards

- Payroll Administration Memorandum #20, 2000-2001: IEP Arbitration Decision

- This document states that when a teacher loses his/her preparation period due to attendance at an IEP conference, this conference shall not be considered as an "emergency." Consequently, the teacher must be compensated.

- UFT Special Education Complaint Form

Copies of IEPs

The IEP describes the school's obligation to provide specially designed instruction as well as related and other support services to students with disabilities. In order for students to achieve the full benefit of the IEP planning process, school personnel with responsibility for implementing the IEPs of students with disabilities must understand their responsibilities and have students' IEPs readily available to them. Chapter 408 of the Laws of 2002 and state regulations prescribe the process for ensuring that this occurs.

Providing Copies of IEPs to Teachers and Related Service Providers

Every principal must implement procedures to ensure that each **general education teacher, special education teacher and related service provider** who is responsible for implementing the student's IEP is provided a **paper or electronic copy** of the IEP **prior to implementation** of the IEP. This includes every teacher responsible for implementing a service, accommodation and/or program modification on a student's IEP. Additionally, a process must be in place to ensure that copies of a student's IEP are immediately disseminated to all appropriate staff when the IEP has been **revised** during the school year.

A school does **not** meet the requirements of the law by disseminating lists of students requiring test accommodations or summaries of IEPs such as "IEP at a Glance."

The determination of which teachers and related service providers must be provided a copy of the IEP should be made at the student's **IEP meeting**.

Teachers of **students who have been declassified** and who continue to receive accommodations, modifications and/or other support services must receive a copy of the student's last IEP.

Providing Paraprofessionals Opportunity to Review and Ongoing Access to IEPs

Every principal must implement procedures to ensure that each paraprofessional responsible for assisting the implementation of a student's IEP is provided the opportunity to **review a copy** of the student's IEP prior to implementation of the IEP.

Additionally, the procedures must ensure that each paraprofessional responsible for assisting in the implementation of a student's IEP has **ongoing access** to a copy of the IEP. The copy may be the copy provided to the student's special education teacher or another teacher or related service provider under whose direction the paraprofessional works. It may also be a copy maintained in another location in the school building if that location is readily accessible to the paraprofessional.

While schools are not required to provide a copy of the IEP to the paraprofessional, they may legally do so if they choose.

Informing School Personnel of IEP Implementation Responsibilities

In addition to providing copies of IEPs to teachers and related service providers and access to paraprofessionals, every principal must have a process for ensuring that each general education teacher, special education teacher, related service provider and other support staff has been informed, prior to implementation of the IEP, of his or her responsibility to implement the recommendations on the student's IEP, including the responsibility to provide specific IEP-mandated accommodations, program modifications, supports and/or services.

To accomplish these, the principal must designate one or more professional staff members who are familiar with the contents of the student's IEP, such as an administrator, school psychologist and/or teacher, to directly inform appropriate staff of their specific responsibilities. Teachers and related service providers who were present at the meeting where the IEP was finalized are assumed to be familiar with the contents of the IEP and their specific duties in implementing the IEP.

Confidentiality

The Federal Educational Rights and Privacy Act (FERPA) allows schools to disclose personally identifiable information in a student's education records, including the student's IEP, to school personnel with "legitimate educational interests." While an IEP contains important instructional information that teachers, related service providers, paraprofessionals and others need to know to implement the IEP, it may also contain sensitive personal information about the student. Teachers and related service providers who receive a copy of a student's IEP and paraprofessionals who have access to IEPs must ensure that student IEPs remain confidential and are not disclosed to any other people.

The school is responsible for instructing all people who receive copies of IEPs or have access to IEPs regarding their legal obligation to maintain the confidentiality of student records. Personally identifiable student information from the IEP may not be disclosed to others without parent consent.

- State Regulations: 8 NYCRR §200.4(e)(3)
- NYC DOE Special Education Annual Review Implementation (with attachment on Chapter 408)
- State Guidance on Providing Copies of IEPs for Students with Disabilities
- This document includes a copy of the law and state regulations.

Providing a Copy of the IEP to Parent

Schools must ensure that a copy of the IEP is provided to the student's parents. If the IEP is amended with or without an IEP team meeting, the parent must be provided with a copy of the amended IEP immediately.

- NYC DOE Standard Operating Procedures Manual, pp. 73 & 109
- State Regulations: 8 NYCRR §200.4(e)(3)(iv)

Storage of IEPs

IEPs are confidential documents and must be kept in locations not accessible by students or staff members who are not responsible for implementing the IEP. While the storage location must not be accessible, this does not necessarily mean that it must be in a locked location.

Questions and Answers from Live Web Cast on the Standard Operating Procedures Manual

Resources

- State Guidance on Providing Copies of IEPs for Students with Disabilities
- This includes a copy of the law and State regulations.
- NYC DOE Special Education Annual Review Implementation (with attachment on Chapter 408)
- Standard Operating Procedures Manual
- State Regulations: 8 NYCRR §200.4(e)
- UFT Special Education Complaint Form

Amending the IEP after the Annual Review

Amendments to an IEP *after* the annual review may be made by the IEP team at an IEP team meeting, or by amending the IEP without an IEP team meeting.

Before an IEP can be amended without an IEP team meeting, the IEP team must clearly describe all proposed changes on the Waiver of IEP Meeting to Amend IEP Form which must include a clear description of all proposed changes, and send the form to the parent. Additionally, the IEP team designee must discuss with the parent any and all changes that are being considered. If the parent needs further information regarding the proposed change(s) or believes that a discussion with the IEP team is necessary before deciding to amend the IEP, the parent does not have to agree to the request to amend the IEP. If the parent does not agree to the proposed changes, the changes cannot be made without an IEP team meeting.

Once the IEP Team receives the signed Waiver of IEP Meeting to Amend IEP, the team may make the changes to the IEP, indicating next to every change the date on which the changes were agreed.

The parent and all staff responsible for implementing the IEP must be provided with a copy of the amended IEP immediately (i.e., The IEP must be sent or otherwise transmitted the following day) and all staff responsible for implementing the changes in the IEP must be informed of their IEP implementation responsibilities.

Additionally, a copy of the signed Waiver of IEP Meeting to Amend IEP must be placed in the student's special education file.

Please Note: An IEP may be amended only after an annual review IEP meeting.

Source: NYCDOE Standard Operating Procedures Manual, pp. 72-73

Chapter II

THE STUDENTS WITH DISABILITIES ESSAY:

Many of my students have told me that their scores on the CST Students with Disabilities go up and down. Sometimes they get a high score and then other times the score is failing. Most students don't know why this happens. Part of the problem is that the teacher writing the essay does not pay attention to the details that matter to the graders of the NYSCTE. The format that I have created for the essay uses the mnemonic device of **SOAP SOUP.** I encourage test takers to practice writing the essay using this format. However, you should be able to create an essay format that is uniquely your own so that you do not receive a **U** on the essay. This format is designed as a practice template to help you identify your strengths and weaknesses.

First we will discuss the common mistakes that teachers make when writing the essay.

Common Mistakes Teacher's Make:

Writing a Teacher Centered Essay

This is a common mistake that teachers make. It is understandable that you feel that you are being asked to explain your abilities as a Special Education teacher and what you think about the topic. But this is wrong.

You will lose major points on the essay if you say "**I**" too much. Think of an IEP. This is basically the format of the essay, a mini IEP. When you write an IEP you don't write it about the teacher, you write it about the student.

Not explaining the diagnosis:

Many teachers make this silly mistake. Part of the CST-SWD test is testing you on your ability to correctly diagnose the disability. Even though the disability is identified in the question it is important for you to explain the behaviors and difficulties that make clear to you that this is the correct diagnosis. If an essay tells you that a student has a Hearing Impairment, you must identify what would indicate this disability e.g.:

Timmy is an 8 year old student in a General Education classroom who has been diagnosed with a hearing impairment. Timmy does not wear a hearing aid but he has difficulty hearing people speaking unless he is able to see their mouth. Although Timmy has good receptive language skills he struggles with his expressive language skills. In addition he often suffers from feelings of isolation from his peers because it is difficult for him to participate in conversations when many people are speaking.

A teacher with a Special Education background should be able to easily diagnose symptoms, behaviors and issues that arise because of a disability. And most teachers can, but for some reason they don't mention them in the essay. This is a very important part of the essay. Don't omit the diagnosis.

I have found an excellent online resource from John's Hopkins University that gives a list of difficulties, teaching strategies and accommodations that are important to know for each disability. They can be found here:

http://web.jhu.edu/disabilities/faculty/guidelines.html or simply Google:

"Guidelines for teaching students with disabilities JHU"

Picking the wrong age:

As we discussed earlier in the book, it is very important to pay attention to the age of the student. Many teachers choose the age they are the most experienced in teaching. This can be a problem if you are not following DOE rules in your classroom. It is important to focus on the stages of Piaget and to keep in mind the way a child's disability can affect these stages. For example, if a teacher was teaching an autistic child and one of the issues was the difficulty an autistic child has with social skills. If a teacher picks a 5-7 year old child and decides on work on the skills they need in cooperative learning groups, this teacher could be making a mistake. A student who is 5-7 years old is in the Pre Operational stage. In this stage a student already struggles with understanding different perspectives and the feelings of their peers. It would be a very difficult and potentially unfair strategy to attempt to work on social skills with a child who is normally in this stage with the added disability of autism. Yet many teachers do this. When you write your essay, after you are finished, be sure to go back and make sure that the age of the student is appropriate for the strategy you plan to use.

If we look at the example on the NYSTCE Preparation Guide for Students with Disabilities, we can see that the age of the student in their example is 14 years old. This is a much different kind of student. Sometimes simply changing the age of the student to an older age, is the difference between a passing or failing the essay. Do not hesitate to change the age of the student if you realize it doesn't match your strategy.

Also try not to mention both the age and the grade in the essay. Stick with the age of the student. You could be accidentally making a mistake about placement without even realizing it. Some special education students are held back a year or two.

Making the disability very severe:

I have no idea why teachers do this. Say you are given "Hearing Impairment" as the disability. There is no reason to make the child deaf or severely hearing impaired. It is to your advantage to make the disability as mild as possible in order to write a very simple essay. When it comes to disabilities like mental retardation and cerebral palsy, it is important to understand that you are attempting to teach the student in a public school classroom. There are a few options you have with your choice of classroom. You can choose: General Education, CTT or Self Contained (Special Education.) But keep in mind that this test is about educating students in the public school system. If the student is severely disabled they will not be able to be taught in a public school classroom. So when possible make the disability a mild form. Notice on the NYSCTE Preparation Guide essay online that they have Sam as a relatively high functioning autistic student. Keep this in mind.

Making the disability too mild

The opposite of this is of course making the disability too mild. This is problematic when discussing learning disabilities and ADD, or ADHD. If a child struggles a little bit in math that is not the same thing as a learning disability. Students who have hyperactivity or behavior issues, need to have a consistent pattern of behavior for it to qualify as ADD. When thinking about these sorts of disabilities it is important that you remember to mention **Frequency, Duration and Intensity.** It is also important to consider the age as well, as we have discussed.

Not being objective in observations:

When you are writing your essay it is basically like writing an IEP. It is important to remember that you cannot use personal and emotional language when discussing the student. Your documentation should always sound objective and give details to support your observations. For example if we say that Timmy has difficulty sitting still in class, we need to add objective details to back up the observations. These details should focus on **Frequency, Duration and Intensity.** You need to discuss how often the behavior happens, how long it lasts and how severe it is. This is an important part of any documentation. It gives vital information to the IEP team. Remember to give objective and detailed observations. You will have to create these observations on your own. But we'll look at some examples later.

Using Methods that are not approved by the DOE:

Keep in mind that when you went to college you learned many different approaches to dealing with the needs of Students with Disabilities. Not all of these are approved by the DOE. For example ABA approach (Applied Behavior Analysis) depends on repetition and doing things over and over again. This is not in compliance with the Constructivist Approach and the DOE. So this is not a strategy that should be used in an essay. Granted you might use this approach in your classroom. But keep in mind that we don't always follow the rules in our classrooms. Keep it safe, only do things approved by the DOE.

Soap Soup

Each of letters in the SOAP SOUP format represents only 1 or 2 sentences. But they are sentences you must include in order to pass the essay. It is important to keep the essay student centered. Do not use the word "I" in the essay. Your job is to write a Mini IEP. You should discuss the student, not the teacher. You should not write the essay as a way of explaining your skills.

Specific

- Student's name
- Student's age
- What type of classroom is the student placed in
- What is the diagnosis

Observations (what behaviors are indicative of diagnosis)

List 2-3 observations and symptoms

Analysis (Choose one of the areas above to examine)

- Frequency
- Duration
- Intensity

Pick **a teacher for collaboration:** Usually one below:

- **General Education Teacher**
- **Occupational Therapist for fine motor skills**
- **Speech Pathologist for language issues**

Specific **Issue to be worked on.** Try for one of the following:

- **Expressive Language Disorder**
- **Organizational or Staying on Task**
- **Social Skills**
- **Fine Motor Skills**
- **Self Advocacy**

Objective **Observations . Always document in details.**

List 2-3 observations

Understanding **how it disrupts with the Student's learning.**

o **How can improving this difficulty contribute positively to the student's learning?**
o **Students strengths and weaknesses**

Plan

- ➢ **Goal for the student**
- ➢ **Assessment if needed**
- ➢ **Accommodations if needed**
- ➢ **Support of collaborating teacher**
- ➢ **Documentation**
- ➢ **Monitoring for Effectiveness**

Let's take a look at an example that follows this format. This is an essay one of my students wrote. The topic was Math Learning Disability. The student received a 260 on the essay:

Carl is 10 year old boy with a Learning Disability in Math who attends 5th grade general education class. Carl is relatively high functioning student who does well in his other subjects but struggles in math. Carl struggles with organizations skills, difficulty in reasoning and understanding logic problems in math. Because of this Carl will often get frustrated during lessons and shut down. He also calls himself "stupid" when he can't understand a concept.

The Special Education teacher and General Education teacher decided to work collaboratively to create a plan of support. It is important for Carl to work on his self-advocacy skills because it will contribute positively to Carl's learning by setting a foundation in ownership of his learning. Self–advocacy will help Carl to collaborate with other students in cooperative learning.

The strategy that will be used will be a journal where Carl will document times during which he is confused and frustrated during math class. He will document the concept that is being discussed as well as how he feels when he is frustrated.

The General Education teacher, Special Education teacher and Carl will meet periodically in order to discuss the things he has written in the journal. It is important for Carl to get immediate and specific feedback to the questions he has written as well as exploring his frustration in feelings. It is important for Carl to understand that asking questions in class is not the mark of an inadequate student but rather a self directed learner.

Furthermore, since Carl enjoys working on a computer, Carl will be rewarded with extra time on the computer for completing his weekly journal entries. In addition, Carl will collaborate with both of his teachers through self-monitory of his own self evaluation journal

The General Education teacher, Special Education teacher and Carl will work together to evaluate and monitor this plan throughout the lesson plan so that it may be modified as necessary.

Why this is a good essay:

> **Student centered and Includes Carl**
> **Explained Diagnosis**

- ➤ **Points out that Carl only has difficulty in math**
- ➤ **Uses Constructivist Approach terminology**
- ➤ **Uses least restrictive environment**
- ➤ **Mentions monitoring the plan**
- ➤ **Recognizes the importance of self evaluation**

Let's look at two similar essays. One is for Cerebral Palsy and the other is for Hearing Impairment:

Sam is a nine year old student in a CTT classroom who has been diagnosed with cerebral palsy. Sam has trouble with body movement, limitations in activity and communication ability. Sam has good receptive language skills but struggles with his expressive language.

One of the areas in which Sam has difficulty is in participating during the cooperative learning parts of the class. It is important for Sam to master his ability to participate in class activities The Occupational Therapist has been working with Sam to support his needs in this area. The strategy that is being used is a touch mouse and laptop. Sam needs to strengthen his finger dexterity so that he will not fatigue easily and can participate fully in class.

The Special Education teacher and Occupational Therapist will work together in order to create a plan of support. To begin the teachers will sit with the Occupational therapist to discuss Sam's needs in this area. Sam will be asked to consider his strengths and weaknesses and his motivation for this behavior. The Occupational therapist will meet Sam two times a week to work on his fine motor skills. These are essential for him to use the touch mouse.

A picture of a Sam participating in the class will be used with the Occupational Therapist as a prompt. The Special Education teacher will use the same picture as a visual reminder. The OT helps Sam to maximize his function, adapt his limitations, and live as independently as possible.

To monitor the effectiveness of this technique, the OT will take anecdotal notes on Sam's session to give observable feedback. The Special Education Teacher will take frequency data on how many times Sam independently participates in the class and how many times he needed a prompt to remind him.

Hint! If you are unfamiliar with the role of the OT or SP you can work with the General Education teacher but write one sentence that shows that the student has been receiving ongoing support from a specialist. The example below uses this strategy by mentioning the Speech Pathologist.

Hearing Impairment:

Marie is a nine year old in a general education classroom who has been diagnosed with a hearing impairment. Marie has difficulty hearing but doesn't use a hearing aid. She has good receptive language skills but struggles with her expressive language skills. She prefers working with the teacher one on one. One of the areas in which she has difficulty is in participating during the collaborative learning part of the class. She withdraws from conversation and will not contribute in group discussion.

It is important for Marie to master her ability to participate during collaborative learning because it will contribute positively to her learning by developing self directed learning and ownership. This will also enable her to participate fully in class. The Speech Pathologist has been working with Marie to support her needs in this area.

The Special Education Teacher and the General Education Teacher will work together to create a plan of support. To begin the teacher will sit with Marie and discuss her needs in this area. Maria will be asked to consider her strengths and weaknesses and her motivations for this behavior. The strategy that will be used will be to have the class work in collaborative groups and during discussion a marble or small ball will be passed around the group prompting each student to take turns contributing to the conversation. This is a good strategy to use because it will not single out Marie, but be activity in which the whole class participates. This is also a good strategy because hearing impaired students benefit from using visual cues to identify when a transition has occurred. In addition the General Education teacher will provide Marie with a transcript of the directions that will be followed in class during the activity.

The General Education Teacher will support Marie by reminding her to participate when she has the ball. She will also encourage Marie to hold the ball longer each time as she improves her expressive language. In addition the General Education teacher will monitor Marie's progress in order to give observable feedback. Together the General Education teacher, Special Education teacher and Marie will work to access progress and to modify the plan as necessary.

Let's look at another essay. This essay received a 300 on the exam. The disability is Autism and the strategy is specific.

Debbie is a nine year old nonverbal girl with autism who attends special education school for full day. Debbie is not able to communicate her thoughts, needs or wants at the same level as her peers. The special education teacher will collaborate with the speech language pathologist.

The speech language pathologist will use PEC (Picture Exchange

Communication System) for Debbie. Debbie will be able to use pictures instead of words to communicate. The speech language pathologist will introduce the picture exchange communication book during her one on one session. Language will be used by the communication partner with pictures.

After speech language pathologist introduces the book to Debbie, she will use it every day at school and home. The speech language pathologist will also train Debbie's parents, other therapist who work with her and her classroom team.

When first learning to use PEC, Debbie is given a set of pictures of favorite foods or toys. When the she wants one of these items, she gives the picture to a communication partner (a parent, therapist, classroom teacher). The communication partner then hands the child the food or toy. This exchange reinforces communication.

For Debbie to initiate more, the communication partner moves slightly away from her so she has to child move towards the communication partner to place the picture card in his/her hand.

To advance Debbie's communication she is given more than one picture card. At this point, the child may be using a communication binder in which to hold the cards. The will be divided into different sections such as food, people, activities, toys. Debbie will choose desired object, and then give this card to the communication partner.

Use of pictures associated with words will help Debbie to be able to communicate her needs and wants without feeling frustration. Pictures can be added and removed as per Debbie's interests and needs.

Phrases to use:

❖ *The special education teacher will collaborate with the _____ _____ in order to create a plan of support.*

❖ One of the areas in which (student) has difficulty is in_____ during *(reading, transitions, physical education, sitting on the rug, independent reading, cooperative learning, math, art class, science, etc.)*

❖ It is important for (Student) to master _____ because it will contribute positively to (Student's) learning by: (*choose one*)

    ➢ setting a foundation in_____
    ➢ developing his or her social skills for collaborative learning
    ➢ encouraging a sense of ownership in learning

❖ Additionally the _____ teacher will monitor (Student's) progress in order to give observable feedback.

❖ Together the _____teacher, Special Education teacher and (Student) will work together to assess progress and to modify the plan as necessary.

Jobs of the Collaborating Teacher:

It is important to keep your essay simple. Remember it is only worth about 10% of the score. It is great if you score high on the essay, but remember I didn't even pass the essay and I passed the exam. Be as prepared as you can but try to keep the collaborations simple. For example, the role of the General Education teacher should basically be to: remind the student to follow the plan, observe the student in the classroom, give observable feedback to the IEP team, and monitor the success of the IEP in order to modify the plan if necessary. You don't need to go into detail.

The Occupational therapist will work with the student, document progress and give feedback to the IEP team.

The Speech Pathologist will work with the student, document progress and give feedback to the IEP team.

When using the OT or the SP, explain the work they will do with the student and then mention "documenting progress" and giving feedback to the IEP team. That's about it!

One final hint. It is acceptable to write the essay from the perspective of the General Education teacher collaborating with the Special Education teacher. I'm not sure why this is acceptable but many of my students have scored above 250 on the essay using this strategy. If you get stuck you can try this approach.

However I would like to point out that this is the easiest essay for which to prepare because you KNOW what the question is going to be. You just don't know which disability they are going to ask about. Keep up to date on the recent test prompts and you should be able to practice pre-writing no more than 4 possible topics when you get to the exam. Good luck!

Chapter 12

CHAIN OF COMMAND AND EDUCATIONAL HIERARCHY IN PUBLIC SCHOOLS AND THE UFT:

The next two sections are filled with legal jargon and densely written information. However you will get about 3-5 questions on the ATS-W and the CST SWD that ask you about the roles and responsibilities in the DOE Educational Hierarchy. Don't feel pressured to understand all of these sections. Try to keep it basic. Just know who is responsible for what. You should not stress yourself out trying to memorize this information. Just try to understand the basics.

The following are the legal obligations of each member of the NYC Department of Education. Please remember that the test you are taking is not for New York City specifically. It is important for NYC teachers to know not only these obligations but also the state obligations. But for the purposes of the exam the most important roles are that of the Principal, Superintendant and Teachers. Those are highlighted in bold below.

(source: http://commongood.org/burdenbook-40.html)

Chain of Command New York City Department of Education

Confused about how the New York City system fits together? Who is in charge? Well, with the changes to the law, it is simpler now than it used to be. Here is a summary:

Mayor

- Hires the Chancellor and appoints 8 of 13 City Board members.

Board of Education or "City Board" or "Panel for Educational Policy"

- Main responsibility: Approve major policy changes (through resolutions); §2590-g:

    o Policy directly related to student achievement;
    o Major educational contracts that would significantly impact the provision of educational services or programming;
    o Collective bargaining agreements;

- Composed of 13 members; §2590-b(1)(a):

    o 5: One appointed by each borough president–member must be a resident of the borough and have a child within the city school district;
    o 7: Appointed by the Mayor–must be a resident of the city;
    o 1: Chancellor–appointed by the Mayor;

- Members serve at the pleasure of the appointing official and shall not be employed in any capacity by New York City;
- Board must have at least twelve meetings per year; §2690-b(1)(b);
- See current members of the Panel for Educational Policy;
- Powers and duties:

- o   Mainly to advise the Chancellor on matters of policy;
- o   Can bring some charges, in accordance with Civil Service Law §75, against employees; Bylaws §4.2.1;
- o   Must define the boundaries of community school districts within the city district every ten years starting in 2004; §2590-b(2)(c);
- o   Redistrict Advisory Study group will study this and make recommendations; process must be public;
- o   The Chancellor is authorized to establish and publish appropriate rules and regulations for the processing of appeals with the approval of the Board; Bylaws §5.1;
- o   Does not supervise the day-to-day operations of any school within the city school district;

- •   The Chancellor can issue an order to any community board and/or superintendent requiring any conduct that the Chancellor believes is improper to cease or take other required action; §2590-l;
- •   Board Meetings:

  - o   Open to the public;
  - o   Quorum: Majority of the members.

Chancellor

- •   Chairperson of the Panel for Educational Policy;
- •   Serves at the pleasure of the Mayor;
- •   Previously served at the pleasure of the Board;
- •   Length of term cannot extend more than two years;
- •   Four volumes of Chancellor's Regulations cover nearly all aspects of public schools. See the Regulations;
- •   Powers and duties; 2590-h:

  - o   Examples: fiscal and educational equity, operate senior high schools and all specialized high schools, school construction oversight, promulgate clear educational standards and curriculum to be periodically evaluated, training programs for principals and employees, develop a parental bill of rights, and transfer of principals. Based on scores, schools are ranked and then must follow rules promulgated by the Chancellor if they fall below a certain level;

o Shall promulgate minimum education and experience requirements for all teaching and supervisory positions; §2590-j(2);

o Shall cause a reading examination to be administered annually to all pupils in all schools in each community district (5a-e);

o If community superintendent causes charges to be brought against an employee, the Chancellor usually determines what action to take; §2590-j(7)(d);

o Can issue an order requiring a community district to cease an activity that violates any law, bylaw, rule, or regulation, etc., in addition to §2590-h; §2590-l(1);

o Community District or superintendent can appeal to the City Board; §2590-l(2);

o Must develop an election process for the parent and parent-teacher associations in each District Education Council (see District education councils above and §2590-h(15)(b-1));

o Prepares an educational facilities master plan and five-year educational facilities capital plans; §2590-p.

Regions or "Instructional Divisions"

- Focus: Implementing the new comprehensive instructional approach;
- There are 10 Instructional Divisions located throughout the city, each covers approximately 120 schools and is led by a Regional Superintendent;
- The offices will be called "Learning Support Center Sites" and will provide a range of services to parents.

Regional Superintendents

- The 10 Regional Superintendents report to the Deputy Chancellor for Teaching and Learning. The Deputy and these 10 will form the senior instructional management team of the school system;
- The current 10 were selected by the Deputy Chancellor on the basis of demonstrated leadership, and the Chancellor made the final decision;
- The 10 new Instructional Divisions will be comprised of groups of 2-4 existing Community School Districts, as well as the high schools located within the geographic boundaries of the divisions;
- Each Regional Superintendent oversees all aspects of instruction for the public school system, including classroom instruction.

Community District Education Councils or "Community Council"; formerly "Community Boards"; §2590-c (2003 N.Y. ALS 123 §3)

- Goal: Encourage greater participation by parents, community residents, and other citizens in local schools;
- There are 32 Community Councils (one community council for each district education council);
- Composed of 12 members (a-c):

   o 9: Parents whose children are attending a school under the jurisdiction of the community district and shall be selected by the presidents and officers of the parents' association or parent-teachers' association. 2 year terms;

   o The Chancellor must develop an election process for election of these associations and must assure process is uniform (8a), meets fair cross-section of the community (8c), and is public;

   o 2: Appointed by borough president. Must be residents of, or own or operate a business in, the district and will make a significant contribution to improving education in the district. 2 year terms;

- o 1: Non-voting high school senior, appointed by the school district superintendent. 1 year term;

- Submit to the City Board a performance report every month (7a);
- Promulgate rules and regulations regarding financial disclosure (8e). Before passing any regulations, the Chancellor must ensure there is a public process to ensure public input;
- Shall prescribe bylaws and regulations §2590-d(2) that must include:

  - o A parents' association (or parent-teachers') in each school §2590-h(15));
  - o Regular communication between Council, community superintendent, and the principal of each school, and at least once per quarter meet with elected officers;
  - o Council develops a process for community input in evaluations of the district superintendent and other supervisors;
  - o Council's duties are largely advisory;
  - o Evaluates district superintendent and other instructional supervisors assigned or appointed to the district by the Chancellor; §2590-d(2c);
  - o Holds monthly meetings with the district superintendent;
  - o Prepares a school district report card and make it publicly available; §2590-e(8).

Community Superintendents; §2590-f

- The Chancellor appoints community superintendents in compliance with certain education, managerial, and administrative qualifications; §2590-h(29, 30);
- Duties: 21 different categories are listed as duties/responsibilities (1, a-u);

- Except supervisors, superintendents appoint, define the duties of, assign, promote, and discharge all employees of the community district, and fixes their compensation and terms of employment, consistent with any collective bargaining agreement §2590-f(1)(c);
- Appoints supervisory personnel from the candidates screened by a committee including parents, teachers, and school support personnel (d);
- Appoints or rejects the principal candidates screened by screening committees (e);
- Evaluates principal's performance, authority to transfer or remove principals, reviews and approves school-based budgets;
- Operates cafeteria or restaurant services for pupils, teachers, the community for school related functions and activities, and the elderly of the district (m);
- Can initiate charges against some employees for certain offenses; §2590-j(7)(b)(1-6).

Schools & Principals; §2590-i

- **The principal is the administrative and instructional leader of an individual school, subject to the Chancellor's Regulations and collective bargaining agreements; the principal is responsible for day-to-day operations of the school;**
- **The principal selects curricula, syllabi, and texts from lists approved by the Chancellor, and subject to superintendent's approval.**

Teachers and Supervisors

- **With the approval of the City Board, the Chancellor promulgates the minimum education and experience requirements for teachers;**
- **The Chancellor appoints and assigns teachers and supervisory personnel for all schools and programs from eligible lists selected at random from qualifying eligible lists (4a, b).**

Miscellaneous

- **New body created: "Citywide Council on Special Education":**

  - **9 members: Parents of special education children;**
  - **2 members: Appointed by public advocate;**
  - **1 member: High school special education student (non-voting);**
  - **2 year terms.**

The roles and responsibilities of the UFT:

(source: http://www.uft.org/)

HINT: The question involving the UFT on the exams is usually asking who represents the teacher in legal issues.

Union Basics

The UFT, which represents approximately 200,000 members, is the sole bargaining agent for most of the non-supervisory educators who work in the New York City public schools. We represent approximately 87,000 teachers and 19,000 classroom paraprofessionals, along with school secretaries, attendance teachers, guidance counselors, psychologists, social workers, adult education teachers, administrative law judges, nurses, laboratory technicians, speech therapists, and 53,000 retired members. We also represent teachers and other employees of a number of and private educational institutions and some charter schools.

The allied Federation of Nurses/UFT represents some 2,800 registered nurses of the New York City Visiting Nurse Service and several private New York City hospitals and health care institutions.

Over 28,000 New York City family child care providers became the UFT's newest members after a successful organizing drive that gained collective-bargaining rights in 2007. Their first contract was ratified in 2010.

UFT Governance Structure

The eleven officers, elected for three-year terms, are the president; six vice presidents selected at large (including one each from elementary, junior high/intermediate, academic high and career and technical high schools and special education); secretary and assistant secretary; treasurer and assistant treasurer. The union has an office in each borough and fields a borough representative for each borough and a district representative for each community school district and high school district.

Each school has a chapter leader elected by the members of that school. In addition, there are "functional chapters" to represent non-teacher members, each with a chapter leader elected citywide.

The UFT has three governing bodies. The 3,400-member Delegate Assembly is the union's legislature, with elected representatives from every school. The 89-member elected Executive Board sets policy on a variety of education, labor and union issues. The Administrative Committee, composed of the eleven officers, borough representatives and selected department heads, oversees day-to-day operations.

UFT Locations

The UFT's central headquarters is located at 50/52 Broadway in Manhattan. There are also UFT offices in each of the five boroughs where members can go to get help with certification, licensing, salaries, grievances and pensions.

Each UFT borough office is open from 10 a.m. to 6 p.m., Monday through Friday, when school is in session. To better serve members, the Bronx, Manhattan and Queens offices are open until 7 p.m. on Thursdays while the Brooklyn and Staten Island offices are open until 7 p.m. on Tuesdays.

Go here for directions to get to UFT headquarters and the UFT borough offices.

UFT Union Affiliations

The UFT was founded in 1960 as Local 2 of the now 1.4 million-member American Federation of Teachers (AFT). Our union is also affiliated with the 600,000-member New York State United Teachers (NYSUT) and a member of the AFL-CIO and the New York City Central Labor Council.

Chapter 13

WHAT KIND OF TEST TAKER ARE YOU?

The Rolling Stones have a hit song that talks about Time being on their side. Unfortunately on the NSTCE tests time is your greatest enemy. It is important to consider time management and to know your strengths and weaknesses. The key is not to rush through the exam but to carefully answer the questions that you often get wrong due to silly mistakes. If you have strength in another section it will help you save time for the ones in which you are weak. It is important to really visualize how much time you actually have on the test. In my class I often will write this on the board:

5 minutes per question @80 questions is 400 minutes. How many hours is that?

Quite often my students will say "4 hours." That is incorrect. The answer is 60 minutes per hour divided into 400 is 6 hours and 40 minutes. If you cut that in half you are down to 3 hours and 20 minutes. And this is without writing the essay. So you should be prepared to spend less than 2 minutes per question. In some cases this will be easy. But others will take quite a long time to answer. So time management is important.

One of the important things you can do is to figure out how you take tests. How do you see the questions? Are you more logical or more emotional. A good source for this would be the Myers Briggs Personality Test. You can find the test at the link below:

http://www.humanmetrics.com/cgi-win/JTypes2.asp

The test is free. It is about 70 questions with yes no answers that are designed to test for four different parts of sixteen characteristics of the way a person sees the world. My personality type is the INTP. This is why I am good at taken tests. I generally will see the question logically. I will not "over-think" the question. And I am confident with my choices and do not go back to change them, with one exception. The one exception in this is in Math. I am not good at math and I always think I am getting the question wrong. My lack of confidence is the thing that caused me to fail the math section on the CST Multi Subject. Let me tell you what happened:

My experience on the CST Multi Subject Math Section:

By the time I went down to take the CST Multi I had been teaching it for about 2 years. I use strategy in the class and encourage my students to learn the basics of math. But I'm not confident about math at all. I do know that over-thinking the question is a major problem for most students in this subarea. So I have told my students over and over and over again, "Do not over think the question!" If you meet any of my students and ask them about this they will probably smile and say "Oh yes she really beat us over the head with that one!"

One of the examples I used in class to illustrate this was this one:

2 4 6 8 10 12 14 16 _____ what's next?

15 30 45 60 75 90 105 _____ what's next?

7 14 21 28 35 42 _____ what's next?

Then I would do this one. This one is not math. I am telling you the answer has nothing to do with math. Don't do math!

4 14 23 34 42 _____ what's next?

I would typically watch the students in the class start to do math. I could see the gears in their minds working it out. I'd see them looking for a pattern by subtracting the numbers from the last one. Then I'd interrupt them by writing the answer on the board. The answer is 47-50 Rockefeller Center. These are the train stops on the F line subway in NYC. I wasn't trying to be sneaky. I was trying to show the students why it is important to follow the directions in the question. You will waste all sorts of time figuring out nothing. And the test makers know you will do this. So they will have an answer that matches the answer you come up with. It will be waiting for you as the wrong answer. This is why it is important not to go beyond the question. Keep it simple!

So when I went down to take the CST Multi, I was armed with many of the answers to questions that students had seen repeated on the test over and over again. One of them I remember clearly. On the question there are four square and rectangular shapes. Two of them are squares, and two are rectangles that have slanted sides. The question asks this "If you wanted to add another shape to this group, what would it have to have in common with the other shapes?" And the answer jumped in my head. I remembered this question. We had discussed it in class. The answer was parallel lines. I had gone over this very answer with my students. The options were:

> A. 95 degree angles
> B. Curves
> C. Two pairs of parallel lines
> D. Equilateral

And I froze. I didn't remember the answer having "two pairs" of parallel lines. That was a little different. Was I mistaken? Had they changed the options? I knew it wasn't curves or 95 degree angles. But I hesitated. Then I thought about it a lot and I concluded that since two sides of two of the parallelograms were not parallel to the sides of the squares then this probably wasn't the correct answer. Even though I knew equilateral usually had something to do with triangles, I picked that as the answer. I got it wrong.

Can you believe I made such a stupid mistake? I knew the answer and I picked the wrong answer anyway? And I failed the Math Section. Take a look at my scores:

English Language Arts	273
Mathematics	188
Science and Technology	257
Social Studies	280
The Fine Arts	263
Health and Fitness	263
Family & Consumer Science & Career Dev	300
Foundations of Reading Essay	300

I spent about 40 minutes on this test as well, including the essay. I just buzzed right through it. My only concern was to merely pass it. Except for the part that I felt insecure about. The math section is the section where I changed my answers, hesitated and got confused. And I knew the answers. I want to make that clear. I knew the answers to the questions because we had discussed them in class. And look what happened! Look at the score. I failed the math section. Imagine if I had this attitude on all the other sections? I would have failed the exam.

If I can teach you anything through this experience, it is to not worry or over think the questions. Approach the questions in a simple way and just find the answer. If you don't then the test makers have gotten you and you will not pass the exam. Do not over think the question. Keep it simple,

Let's look at some strategies for the CST Multi Subject exam.

Chapter 14

THE CST MULTI MULTIPLE CHOICE SUBAREAS

The Subareas:

1. English Language Arts. Approx. 21%

2. Mathematics. Approx. 18%

3. Science and Technology Approx. 13%

4. Social Studies Approx. 15%

5. The Fine Arts Approx. 8%

6. Health and Fitness Approx. 8%

7. Family & Consumer Science & Career Dev Approx. 7%

8. Foundations of Reading (Constructed Response: ESSAY) Approx. 10%

The Lowest Percentage Subareas:

The sections that have the lowest percentage of the overall score are the Health and Fitness and Family and Consumer Science and Career Development sections. Usually on the exam there are only 3-5 questions in each of these sections. This means that you have a higher probability of failing this section if you get even one question wrong. Because of the low percentage of these scores and the ability for most students to study these sections on their own I will not cover them in this book. They will not help you pass the exam. You will not fail the exam if you do not pass these sections only. As a test prep coach, my job is to focus on the sections that are essential to pass the exam. Please use the resources at the end of the book to look up any questions that you do not understand. Additionally you may sign up for the online pages which address many of these questions on our website.

The English Language Arts Section:

This is the most important subarea. This section will be discussed in this book after the section on the essay. This section is not necessarily about English or Writing as we would commonly think of it. It is instead about teaching English Language Arts to students. Questions in this section will rely on the Constructivist Approach, The Trap Words to Avoid, Understanding basic Phonics and Reading skills and Important Children's books used in the classroom. These are all covered in detail in the last section. I place this last because by learning all the other strategies and information about the essay first, it is easier to prepare for this subarea.

Mathematics:

Basic Math Terms and Strategies:

The simplest type of math question you can get on the exam is one that asks you to add and subtract a series of long numbers. Test takers usually get pretty excited when they see these types of questions because you know you will be able to figure out the answer. And so you happily waste a lot of time sorting out these answers. However there is actually a simple strategy that turns this into a 2 second question instead of 30 second question.

Let's look at some examples:

The Chester Hill School District has been examining the records of student enrollment for 2009-2010. At the beginning of the school year in September of 2009 there were 2,534,807 students enrolled in the district. By January of 2010-235, 206 students had dropped out. In April 2010-261, 894 students had enrolled. How many students were enrolled in the school by the end of the year?

    A.   2,561,495
    B.   2,299,601
    C.   2,570,493
    D.   2,547,489

This seems easy enough:

$$2,534,807$$
$$-$$
$$235,206$$
$$\text{Equals} \quad 2,299,601$$
$$+$$
$$261,894$$
$$\text{Equals} \quad 2,561,495$$

That is answer A

The thing is, we didn't need to do all that. In addition it is easy to make a careless mistake her by writing the numbers in the wrong order. In fact answer C is the answer if you were to accidentally transpose the numbers 3 and 4 in the original number of students. 2,543,807. If you make this kind of mistake you would do the equation completely wrong and the answer would be right there waiting for you.

Instead the simple way to answer these types of questions is to look at the very last digit in each of the answers. We look to see we have 5 1 3 and 9. The numbers are all different. Just look straight down the last column in the answers. Now all we need to do is a very simple math problem and take the last digit in each of the numbers given: like so

2,534,80 **7**

-

235,20 **6**
_____

Equals 2,299,60 **1**

+

261, 89 **4**

Equals 2,561,49 **5**

A.   2,561,49**5**
B.   2,299,60**1**
C.   2,570,49**3**
D.   2,547,48**9**

By only looking at the last digit we can see that the answer must have the number 5 as the last digit. There is only one answer in the options that does: Answer A. Therefore answer A must be the correct answer. We are done. We have turned a 30 section question into a 2 second question.

PEMDAS and Pythagorean

Most people learn PEMDAS in school. It is the order of operations that must be followed when doing multiple steps to solve an equation. This stands for:

- Parenthesis
- Exponents
- Multiply
- Divide
- Add
- Subtract

PEMDAS is important to remember on the CST Multi because of the exponents more than any other issue. Exponents are shorthand for repeated multiplication of the same thing by itself. For instance, the shorthand for multiplying three copies of the number 5 is shown on the right-hand side of the "equals" sign in $(5)(5)(5) = 5^3$. The "exponent", being 3 in this example, stands for however many times the value is being multiplied. The thing that's being multiplied, being 5 in this example, is called the "base".

The most common question I have seen on the exam that involves order of operations and Exponents are the "walking" or "traveling" questions. They will usually talk about a person traveling a certain amount of miles in one direction, then making a left or right turn and traveling another amount of miles, and then deciding to take a direct line back to the original start point. Sometimes the question will involve a friend walking to see his other friends. It might be a woman walking or jogging through town. It might also be a person driving to another town. What most of these equations are doing is creating a "right triangle." The importance of this is that the solution to the question will require the use of Pythagorean's theorem which states:

In algebraic terms, $a^2 + b^2 = c^2$ where **c** is the hypotenuse while **a** and **b** are the legs of the triangle.

In the word problems, the "hypotenuse" is the "shortest distance back" and the legs of the triangle are the two distances already traveled and given in the equation. So you might get an equation that reads like this:

Fiona sisters live in two neighboring towns. Tamika lives in Townesville which is 30 miles north. First Fiona will pick up Tamika by driving 30 miles north. Then she heads east for another 40 miles to pick up her sister Lydia. After this Fiona drives all the sisters back to her home for the weekend, taking the shortest distance possible. How far does Fiona drive when she returns with her sisters?

    A.   48 miles
    B.   50 miles
    C.   65 miles
    D.   70 miles

Using the Pythagorean theorem the answer is pretty simple to find.

$$30^2 + 40^2 = \underline{\hspace{2cm}}$$

However if you don't follow PEMDAS you can make a mistake. Many students mistakenly ADD first. In this case the answer would be D. 30 + 40 = 70. However the order of operations lets us know that we need to do the Exponents first. So 30 x 30= 900 and 40 x 40= 1600. 900 + 1600= 2500 and so the square root of 2500 is 50. The answer is B.

Area or Perimeter type questions.

Another typical type of question involves figuring out the area of the perimeter of a space. In these types of questions keep in mind that: fences, bleachers around a field, gates, wall paper around a room etc. are questions about Perimeter. To figure out the perimeter you simply add up all the sides.

Area is how much is inside the space. These questions might be things like putting down carpeting, mowing the grass, filling a swimming pool. These are figured out by using length x width.

Odd shaped pictures will usually give you enough information to deduce the missing numbers by subtracting or adding provided information, from the odd shaped side.

One example that they often give is a swimming pool with a semicircle at the end of the pool. To solve this you combine the area or perimeter of the rectangle with the ½ of the area or circumference of the circle. The diameter of the circle is equal to the line at the opposite end of the rectangle. Once you have the diameter (the line that goes all the way across the circle) then you can figure out the radius by dividing the diameter in half. Then you can solve for area or perimeter.

Circumference

The Circumference is the distance around the edge of the circle.

It is exactly Pi (the symbol is π) times the Diameter, so:

$$\text{Circumference} = \pi \times \text{Diameter}$$

Area

The area of a circle is π times the Radius squared, which is written:

$$A = \pi \times r2$$

Pi (the symbol is π) is about equal to 3.14. Just remember that your answer will be a little more than $3 \times r^2$

Let's say the Diameter is 10

Circumference equals about 3.14 x 10 or about 32

Area equals about 3.14×5^2 (3.14 x 25) or a little more than 75

Estimating Odds or Probability

I have never forgotten the first question I ever took on any of the NYSTCEs. It was on the LAST and it was this long complicated question with a chart showing how many times John flipped a coin. How many times did it come up heads. How many times did it come up tails. Then the question was "If John flips a coin again, according the information on the chart above, what are the odds that the coin will come up tails."

I sat there for a moment shocked at the way they had set up the question. Every time you flip a coin the odds are 50/50 or ½. Sometimes on these exams they give you the simplest question and then confuse you by adding all this unnecessary information. When asked to estimate odds you should keep it simple.

Let's look at some examples:

Zuker's Emporium sells gobstoppers that come in different colors. To choose a color you must spin a wheel on the outside of the barrel that contains the candies. The colors are red, green and yellow. Olivia spins the wheel several times. The first spin is green, the second spin is yellow, the third spin is red, the fourth spin is green, the fifth spin is yellow. If Olivia spins the wheel again, what are the odds that the color will be yellow?

A.   1/4
B.   1/3
C.   2/3
D.   2/4

If she's spinning a wheel that has three choices, each time she spins the wheel the probability is 1 out of three chances it will be yellow. All the extra information about how many times she spun the wheel is completely useless information. Do not be fooled by these types of questions. It is always 1 in the number of options. If there were four colors in this question the answer would be ¼. If there were five colors the answer would be 1/5.

You will also need to remember to reduce the probability number to the lowest number. So for example:

Petra's Dance Studio is setting up dance groups for their annual modern movement recital. Students are being chosen for each dance group. There are 6 boys and 6 girls in the studio. Three boys have already been chosen. When Petra chooses another dancer, what are the odds that it will be a boy?

We can do the simple odds here. There are 3 boys left to be chosen and there are 6 girls left to be chosen. That gives us 9 students in total, and of the 9 three are boys. So the odds are 3/9. But we need to reduce it to the lowest number and so the answer is 1/3.

Fractions

Fractions often come up on the exam when you are asked to reduce or reevaluate percentages. A good example of this is using the question that is like a "recipe" where the chef runs out of a certain item and must then adjust the rest of the recipe. For example:

Tony's pizza has been busy all afternoon. Tony wants to make another pie for his last customer but finds he only has three cups of flour left. The recipe consisted of 6 cups of flour and ¼ cup of yeast. Tony decides to make a smaller pie. In order to balance the recipe how much yeast should he use?

A.   ½ cup
B.   7 teaspoons
C.   1/8ᵗʰ a cup
D.   3/16ᵗʰ a cup

The answer is C. It is important to study the fractions and the way they reduce and the way they divide. You can use the links provided at the end of the book to practice these skills.

Word Problems:

This section will have a series of basic math questions written out as word problems. The number one problem that test takers have in this section is that they don't answer the question that was actually asked. The second problem they have is in making careless mistakes. Let's look at an example:

The Duncan Hills organic produce farm sells a variety of pumpkins, squash and gourds. The set price for each type is 49 cents a pound. The specialty items for the month of October include the following: Acorn, Queensland Blue Winter Squash, Baby Boo Pumpkin, Butternut, Calabash, Chayote, Cucumber, Gooseneck, Hubbard, Kabocha, Pattypan, and Pumpkin. These types sell for 34% off the normal set price. To the nearest cent for how much do the pumpkins sell per pound?

A.   66 cents
B.   17 cents
C.   49 cents
D.   32 cents

This type of question is very typical. As you can see there is a lot of "filler" information that has nothing to do with the actual question. In addition the question can be a bit confusing to test takers for whom English is not the native language. The types of squash are confusing and often sound strange. It distracts the test taker from the actual question. The actual question is "How much is the pumpkin after the discount?" But what often happens is that students only do half the math. For example:

If we do the math here we will do:

49 cents times 34% off. We will then get the answer as .1666. If we round this up we get 17 cents. Then we look and see that the answer B is 17. And this is the wrong answer. The answer is D, 32 cents. Why?

In doing the math we forgot to take it to the next step. We are not being asked, how much is the discount? We are being asked, how much is the new price *after* the discount? So we need to subtract the 17 cents from the 49 cents and then we get the answer: 32 cents.

Now this is a very simple question that has been cluttered up by the wording in the question. Be careful and try to use strategy to answer the question.

Strategy 1.
When you see lots of description in the question your red flags should go up and warn you that this is a distraction. This is done deliberately by the test makers to confuse you. Learn to ignore all the extra detail and pull out only the information that pertains to the actual math in the question.

Strategy 2
Use "shoppers math" to answer the question. Shoppers math is what you do when you have a certain amount of money to spend and you want to make sure you are not buying more than you can afford. Shoppers math includes things like:

> ➤ Rounding up or down
> ➤ At least, about
> ➤ less than or more than
> ➤ Using money percentages to help figure out the answer: 10%. 20%. 25%, 33% (a third off), 50%, (half off) 75% etc.

Let's do the same problem using shoppers math. The pumpkins are 49 cents per pound. They want to know how much it would cost if it was 34% off. If we round 34% down we get 33%.

Let's think of a way to make it easier: 49 cents and $1/3^{rd}$ off is close to but more than 45 cents minus 15 cents.

Then if we say that the amount is about a third off, we can simply subtract about 15 cents from 45 cents and get the answer as about 30 cents. The answer will be more than 30 cents but close to 30 cents.

We do this quickly in our minds. Then when we look at the answers we see that only one answer comes close to 30 cents.

    A.   66 cents
    B.   17 cents
    C.   49 cents
    D.   32 cents

But what it the answers are a little different? What if they have the answers this way:

    A.   29 cents
    B.   11 cents
    C.   39 cents
    D.   32 cents

In this case there are several answers close to 30 cents. However we see that it must be "more than" 30 cents and close to 30 cents. This also rules out 29 as too low and 39 as too high.

This kind of strategy takes longer to explain than it actually takes to do. You want to practice deconstructing the questions to see if you can use basic shoppers math to quickly come up with the answer.

If you prefer to do it using the math, remember to be careful to make sure you are actually answering the question that was asked.

These are just some basic strategies I have seen for typical types of questions. You can register online for more questions similar to these and to use the practice links we have compiled. Or you can look them up yourself by looking up practice links online.

Just remember, answer the question they are actually asking, keep it simple and don't over think the question *Good luck!*

Science:

Most students pass this section without the need for strategy. The science sections on any test are usually easy because they rely on literal comprehension. Most Science questions will show you a diagram or chart and ask you what this information means. Comprehending charts is a skill that is difficult to teach in test prep books because if you have difficulty comprehending written information and diagrams then you would probably need assistance from a tutor. Strategies for the science questions include:

- Reading the title of the chart

- Understanding the relationship between the information outline and the information given.

- Knowing your basic science systems and how they work.

As the saying goes "This isn't rocket science" it is simply common sense used with the ability to read information correctly.

Most people panic a bit at the idea of science but do rather well on the exam. If you have failed the science section in the past, I would recommend using Wikipedia for the sections in science with which you struggle. If you struggle with reading comprehension there are some strategies you might find useful. The key to understanding science passages is outlined in the next section. The one area you should know prior to taking the exam are Newton's Laws of Motion:

I. **Every object in a state of uniform motion tends to remain in that state of motion unless an external force is applied to it.**

II. The relationship between an object's mass m, its acceleration a, and the applied force F is $F = ma$. Acceleration and force are vectors (as indicated by their symbols being displayed in slant bold font); in this law the direction of the force vector is the same as the direction of the acceleration vector.

III. For every action there is an equal and opposite reaction.

Chapter 15

DECONSTRUCTING READING COMPREHENSION QUESTIONS

It is important for test takers to be aware of the strategy and self assessment needed to help score high on tests that contain reading comprehension questions.

It becomes easier when we realize that there is a pattern to these sections. Not only is there a pattern but there are only a certain number of possible types of questions that can be asked during a timed, multiple choice test. Many students spend too much time trying to study information that is then not reflected on the actual test. In order to succeed it is important for test takers to employ the following approach.

- ➤ Know the type of passage you are reading

- ➤ Decide if the question is a literal, inferential, or an application type question.

- ➤ Know what types of questions you are good at taking.

- ➤ Practice skills on the types of questions that you are not good at taking.

- ➤ Diagnose the actual question

➢ Learn how to guess properly

Know the type of passage you are reading.

In general there are four types of passages you will be expected to read:

✓ **Social Sciences:** These passages are generally history related. They discuss an era of importance in history or ideologies and famous theorists associated with these ideologies. Examples would be: The Civil Rights Movement, Dr. Martin Luther King Jr, Eleanor Roosevelt, Aristotle, Plato, Religious theorists, Social activists, Political activists etc. Memoirs, diary entries or letters.

✓ **Sciences:** These passages are generally science related and require no prior knowledge to read and comprehend. Usually these types of passages explain an experiment or an animal or a scientific theory.

✓ **Prose fiction:** Poetry, Personal Essay, Short story, Descriptive writing. These passages will generally ask "inferential" questions regarding the character development or poet's point of view. Questions also involve vocabulary.

✓ **Humanities:** These passages are generally critics on something in society or, art, writers, famous works in history, meta-fiction. They will ask you to comprehend the point of view of the writer which is usually an opinion that differs from the common view.

Decide if the question is literal, inferential or application/evaluative

Literal, Inferential and Evaluative Questions

Literal, Inferential and Evaluative questions are the three main sections of a comprehension task. It is regularly used to assess the level of a person's comprehension skill. Literal is mainly the easiest group, Inferential is the medium level and the Evaluative is the difficult part. However, some people do not consider these as these levels. It depends on their comprehension skills.

Literal–A question that can be answered directly from the text. The answer is already there. It is just if you can identify it. Sometimes you would need to word it.

Inferential–A question that cannot be answered straight from the text. You will need to think about it and read over the text to see. The text only tells you hints and clues. Sometimes you would need to word it.

Evaluative–Evaluative questions are very similar to Inferential Questions. However, Evaluative sort of sums up the text and ask you to judge something of the text such as; the meaning, truth, answer, opinion and etc. Sometimes you would need to word it.

TEXT EXAMPLE—

Joseph pulled on his overalls, picked up his milk bucket and headed out to see the cows. The sky was still dark but he could see the violet hue creeping up on the horizon. Dawn would be at 5:30 and the roosters would crow and startle everyone in the house awake. They were used to it by now, they called Red their alarm clock. But that wouldn't happen for an hour. For now it was quiet. Joseph trudged slowly through yard in the brisk pre-dawn air. The dew made everything moist and a light fog hovered several inches above the ground. When he got to the barn he heard the animals begin to move around mooing and making noise. It always amazed him how they could tell he was coming. He opened the heavy wooden door and headed in to the cows.

Literal:

1. What did Joseph wear in the morning.

Joseph wore overalls. (Direct answer is on the text)

2. What animal was Joseph going to see?

Joseph was headed out to see the cows. (Answer already on the text)

Inferential:

1.   What time is it when Joseph does this?

It was 4:30 in the morning. (Using the hints on the text. It says dawn is at 5:30 and that it was an hour from now)

2. What was Joseph going to do with the cows?

Joseph was going in to milk the cows. (Using the hints on the text))

3. Where does Joseph live?

He lives on a farm. (Using hints on the text)

Evaluative:

1.   How did the cows know that Joseph was coming?

Evaluative questions ask you to think about questions that are not explained in the text. So in this case you would think about information you already know or may have read elsewhere. Your answer might be something like:

Animals have a strong sense of smell and also a sensitivity to people coming up to them that is from years of evolutionary development as protection against predators.

When answering a fact question, read both the passage providing the data–and several lines before it–carefully. When a fact question directs you to look at a particular line of text for information, you will often find that one of the answer choices is a deceptive one, taken directly from that line number. More likely than not, there will be something in the sentence or two before the referenced line number that will give you the proper frame for interpreting the data–and hence direct you to the right answer to the fact question.

Don't jump to conclusions with fact questions using Roman numerals to identify answer choices. You will recognize this style of question as soon as you see it:

a. I only
b. II only
c. III only
d. I and II only
e. II and III only

The catch is that, oftentimes, facts I and II will be presented very close to each other in the passage, but fact III will be buried much further in the text. Take the time to review and consider each fact on its own merits. The best strategy for these types of questions is to seek to eliminate the wrong answer rather than searching for the correct one.

In addition be mindful of answers that state "Cannot be determined from the information given." This is not the same as "I don't' know." If you don't know the answer that doesn't mean it cannot be determined. Do not choose this answer unless you truly know that it is the correct answer.

Eliminate the "oohs and ahhs" answer choices. When consultants refer to "oohs and aahs," they are talking about interesting factoids that spice up presentations without adding anything of real value to the analysis. These tests also contain these types of answer choices. An 'ooh and ahh' choice will refer to a fact in the passage . . . but just not to one that answers the question being asked.

Pay Attention to Same Language Trap. Same language trap is "same words different idea." If the question is a literal question the words will usually be the same. But on an inferential question they are usually asking you to paraphrase the idea in different words. If you know the question is inferential then the answer will probably not use identical words in the passage and the answer.

Look for Over-thinking Over-thinking means that the answer seems like a clever case of deduction when in fact it is an assumption that cannot be backed up by the passage itself. Here is an example question that uses over-thinking to confuse the reader:

The train to Baltimore left Penn Station at 4:30 on the dot. Jesse arrived at Penn Station at 4:45.

Based only on the information above, which of the following statements is a valid conclusion?

    A.   **Jesse expected the train's departure to be late.**

    B.   **The conductors of the train like to keep a tight schedule.**

    C.   **Jesse missed his train by five minutes.**

    D.   **If Jesse had taken a taxi instead of the subway he wouldn't have missed the train.**

    E.   **If Jesse did not miss his train, he was not supposed to be on the train to Baltimore.**

Many people make the mistake of picking C as the correct answer. This is due to over-thinking and personalizing the question with our own experiences. We read a question about missing a flight and we think of times we almost missed a flight or train or car ride because we showed up late. However nothing in the above sentences indicates that this was Jesse's train. For all we know he could have shown up at 4:45 to catch a 5 o'clock train. The correct answer is E. Don't get tricked into assuming.

Extreme words.

Some extreme words that are often used on a test to confuse test takers are ones that overstate or understate the point of the writing.

Always, never, only, must, none, forever, exactly, precisely, identical . . .

Main idea or purpose questions The best place to gather the main idea of an essay is in the first paragraph, especially the last line of the first paragraph which will typically involve the thesis statement. Read this paragraph carefully and be careful to use the

Know what types of questions you are good at taking.

This is probably the most important part of the test. When we study we have tendency to "stick with what we're good at doing" rather than strengthening our weaker areas. When you take practice tests, be sure to keep track of areas of strength and weakness. This is essential on a timed test because you can go straight to the areas of strength and speed through these questions and then return to those which require more dedication on your part.

Look out for Mind Bombs

What are Mind Bombs? Mind bombs are questions placed strategically on the exam that are used to throw test takers off. These questions require a great deal of thought to answer but the solution is usually based on a simple idea or formula. The questions are usually placed between two simple questions and are used to disrupt your pacing and cause you to get subsequent answers wrong. What a mind bomb will do is blow your mind up and cause it to become confused and frustrated. Keep something important in mind. Mind bomb questions are worth the same amount of points as the other questions. If you see a mind bomb question, instead of freaking out say "Aha! It is the mind bomb question, I'm going to guess and come back later." Chances are when you come back later you will see the answer more easily.

Don't be afraid to guess. There are several questions on the exam that will take up too much of your time to answer. You will find that if you guess, and return the question after the pressure is off, the answer will be quite simple. Example:

In the code below, each letter represents one syllable. The letters are not necessarily listed in the correct order.

CD = "befit"

FD= "fitful"

FH= "vengeful"

JH= "revenge"

MP= "misuse"

FP= "useful"

What letters are needed to write the code for the word "misfit"?

A CF

B CD

C DP

D MD

E CM

The answer here is D. However if you cannot understand the question just pick an answer and go back later. You will usually find these questions positioned after a series of simple questions. They are designed to throw the test taker off track. Always choose an answer and note on the test question page which answers you'd like to go back to later. DO NOT SKIP. Many people make a mistake of filling the next answer into that space and it throws off all of your answers. Be sure to periodically check to make sure the answer you are filling in on the question sheet matches the number of the question on the question page.

Chapter 16

HISTORY AND SOCIAL STUDIES:

On the next few pages you will find information that is important to know for the exam. I will not explain the information. I will simply high light the information. Most of the questions on the CST Social Studies subarea are simple and direct. However links will be provided if you feel that you need to know more information. Also as an educator I find many of these topics fascinating. One video that I use in the class is on You-tube and discusses 1968. This video covers that year and how it impacted the United States. Many of my students have watched the video several times just for their own personal enjoyment.

But for the purposes of the exam, my job is to help you pass. Not to educate you. You should definitely know the Bill of Rights, which is listed below. You also should take a look at certain years that are bolded below as especially important.

A.D. 1000 Norse seaman Leif Ericsson lands in Newfoundland, which he calls Vinland. Viking ship

1492 Spanish explorer Christopher Columbus makes first voyage to America. He lands in the Bahamas.

1513 Spanish explorer Juan Ponce de León makes his voyage to America landing in Florida.

1607 First American colony is settled in America: Jamestown.

1620 Mayflower arrives in Massachusetts and settles The Plymouth Colony made up by Puritans escaping religious persecution in Europe.

1754-1763 French and Indian War:

1770 Tensions arise between settlers and Britain. Troops fire at settlers in what is known as the Boston Massacre

1773 To protest against taxes, settlers dress up as Indians and board three ships dumping tea overboard. This event is known as the Boston Tea Party.

1774 First meeting of Congress in Pennsylvania.

1775-1783 American Revolution: War of Independence

1776 The Declaration of Independence is written and adopted by Congress.

1777 The first Constitution known as the "Articles of the Confederation" is adopted by Congress.

1789 George Washington is elected president.

1790 The US Supreme Court is established.

1791 Bill of Rights is established. The Bill of Rights are 10 Amendments to the constitution. They are as follows:

> **Amendment I**
> Freedoms, Petitions, Assembly
> Congress shall make no law respecting an establishment of religion, or prohibiting the free exercise thereof; or abridging the freedom of speech, or of the press, or the right of the people peaceably to assemble, and to petition the Government for a redress of grievances.

Amendment II
Right to bear arms
A well regulated Militia, being necessary to the security of a free State, the right of the people to keep and bear Arms, shall not be infringed.

Amendment III
Quartering of soldiers
No Soldier shall, in time of peace be quartered in any house, without the consent of the Owner, nor in time of war, but in a manner to be prescribed by law.

Amendment IV
Search and arrest
The right of the people to be secure in their persons, houses, papers, and effects, against unreasonable searches and seizures, shall not be violated, and no Warrants shall issue, but upon probable cause, supported by Oath or affirmation, and particularly describing the place to be searched, and the persons or things to be seized.

Amendment V
Rights in criminal cases
No person shall be held to answer for a capital, or otherwise infamous crime, unless on a presentment or indictment of a Grand Jury, except in cases arising in the land or naval forces, or in the Militia, when in actual service in time of War or public danger; nor shall any person be subject for the same offence to be twice put in jeopardy of life or limb, nor shall be compelled in any criminal case to be a witness against himself, nor be deprived of life, liberty, or property, without due process of law; nor shall private property be taken for public use, without just compensation.

Amendment VI
Right to a fair trial
In all criminal prosecutions, the accused shall enjoy the right to a speedy and public trial, by an impartial jury of the State and

district wherein the crime shall have been committed; which district shall have been previously ascertained by law, and to be informed of the nature and cause of the accusation; to be confronted with the witnesses against him; to have compulsory process for obtaining witnesses in his favor, and to have the assistance of counsel for his defense.

Amendment VII
Rights in civil cases
In Suits at common law, where the value in controversy shall exceed twenty dollars, the right of trial by jury shall be preserved, and no fact tried by a jury shall be otherwise re-examined in any Court of the United States, than according to the rules of the common law.

Amendment VIII
Bail, fines, punishment
Excessive bail shall not be required, nor excessive fines imposed, nor cruel and unusual punishments inflicted.

Amendment IX
Rights retained by the People
The enumeration in the Constitution of certain rights shall not be construed to deny or disparage others retained by the people.

Amendment X
States' rights
The powers not delegated to the United States by the Constitution, nor prohibited by it to the States, are reserved to the States respectively, or to the people.

1793   Eli Whitney invents cotton gin. This device increased the demand for slaves. George Washington is elected again.

1797   John Adams is elected as the second president

1800   African American slave Gabriel Prosse is hanged for organizing a protest against slavery.

1801   Thomas Jefferson is elected third president.

1803   Louisiana Purchase: United States purchases a French territory in the Midwest from Napoleon for 15 million dollars. It is considered one of the most significant land purchases in history. (Be sure to look this up on the internet to get an understanding of how big this territory actually was. It is much bigger than what we'd consider Louisiana today.)

1804   Lewis and Clark begin their journey to find a waterway that extends across America to the West Coast. They are assisted by a Native American woman named Sacagawea.

1805   Thomas Jefferson elected as president a second time.

1809   James Madison is elected as president.

1812-1814   War of 1812: is a war between the US and Britain over shipping issues. Damage is done to the White House and Capitol when they are set on fire by British troops. Star Spangled banner is written by Francis Scott Key

1814   War is ended with the signing of the Treaty of Ghent

1817   James Monroe is elected as fifth president

1819   Florida is ceded to the US by Spain.

1820   Slavery issues are causing issues between "slave states" and "free states." Slavery is forbidden in the territory purchased during the Louisiana Purchase but Missouri is admitted as a slave state in what is known as The Missouri Compromise. Massachusetts is admitted as a free state in exchange.

1821   James Monroe is elected president again.

1822   Another slave revolt is planned and discovered. Denmark Vesey, an African American slave who had purchased his freedom is hanged with others in South Carolina.

1823   Monroe Doctrine: President Monroe declares that the American continent can no longer be colonized by European countries. 1824

1825   The Erie Canal is opened, linking Lake Erie to the Hudson River. John Quincy Adams is elected as the sixth president.

1828   First public railroad begins construction in the US. The B&O Railroad (the Baltimore and Ohio Railroad)

1829   Andrew Jackson is elected as seventh president

1830   President Jackson signs the Indian Removal Act. I would recommend watching the video links listed at the end of the book to learn more about this. This Act authorized the forced removal of Native Americans from Tennessee and other Eastern States, to Mississippi., It was a violent and traumatic experience.

1831   Another slave uprising is planned and this time is performed. African American slave Nat Turner who organized the revolt is hanged in Virginia as a result.

1833   Jackson's second inauguration (March 4).

1836   Texas declares its independence from Mexico. Bloody battle of the Almo occurs.

1837   Martin Van Buren is elected as the eighth president

1838   The Indian Removal Act continues to remove Native Americans from their land. In a forced removal known as the Trail of Tears, Cherokee are forced from Georgia to Oklahoma. Many of the Native Americans die from illness and starvation. Nearly 4,0000.

1841   William Henry Harrison is elected as the ninth president. When he dies a short time later, Vice President John Taylor is inaugurated.

1845   Manifest Destiny is held as a belief that the U.S. has a right to expand across the entire continent.

1845   The debate over slavery continues as Southerners block The Wilmot Proviso which is introduced to try to ban slavery in territories gained in the Mexican War

1846-1848   Mexican War: U.S. declares war on Mexico in effort to gain California and other territory in Southwest (May 13, 1846). War

1848   War ends. Treaty of Guadalupe Hidalgo is signed. Rio Grande becomes border between Texas and Mexico. California, Nevada, Utah and parts of Colorado, Arizona, Wyoming and New Mexico are given to the US in an agreement of 15 million dollars.

1848   Gold Rush begins in California.

1848   Seneca Falls Convention meets in NY to discuss women's rights and the role of women in society. Elizabeth Cady Stanton is a speaker.

1849   Zachary Taylor is elected as the 12th president

1849   African American slave Harriet Tubman escapes to the north and works with the Underground Railroad, a system designed to help other slaves to escape.

1850   Vice President Millard Fillmore is inaugurated as President after the death of Zachary Taylor.

1850   The Compromise of 1850   helps to establish a crackdown on fugitive slaves. Slave trade is banned in Washington DC.

1852   Uncle Tom's Cabin by Harriet Beecher Stowe's is published. This novel is historically relevant for its influence on the dialogue regarding slavery.

1854   The Missouri Compromise of 1820   is repealed. The issue of slavery continues to create tensions throughout the U.S.

1857   James Buchanan is elected as the 15th president

1857   Dred Scott v. Sanford: Supreme Court rules that slaves are not citizens. Revokes the right of states to ban slavery.

1860   Abraham Lincoln is elected president

1860   South Carolina secedes from the Union (Dec. 20).

1861   Southern states create the Confederate States of American and secede from the Union. These states include Mississippi, Florida, Alabama, Georgia, Texas and Louisiana

1861-1865   The North and South begin the Civil War: Conflict over the issue of slavery. North is called the "Union" and South is called the Confederacy. *Key Battles and Important names include: Union General William T. Sherman who captured and set fire to Atlanta Georgia. General Ulysses S. Grant captured the capital of the Confederacy at Richmond, Virginia Confederate General Robert E. Lee surrendered at the Appomattox Courthouse. Battle of Gettysburg. was the battle with the largest number of casualties in the American Civil War[6] and is often described as the war's turning point.*

1863   Emancipation Proclamation is passed freeing slaves in Southern States.

1863   The Gettysburg Address is famously delivered by President

1863   Settlers are able to claim ownership of land on which they have lived for five years as the Homestead Act is passed.

1865   Lincoln is assassinated (April 14) by John Wilkes Booth in Washington, DC, and is succeeded by his vice president, Andrew Johnson.

1865   The Constitution is amended prohibiting slavery. This is the Thirteenth Amendment.

1868   President Johnson is impeached by the House of Representatives (Feb. 24), but he is acquitted at his trial in the Senate (May 26).

1865   The Constitution is amended to define citizenship. This is the Fourteenth Amendment

1869   Ulysses S. Grant is elected as the 18th president (March 4).

1870   The Constitution is amended to give African Americans the right to vote. This is the Fifteenth Amendment

1873   Grant's second inauguration

1876   The Battle of the Little Bighorn, also known as Custer's Last Stand was an armed engagement between combined forces of Native American Indians –Lakota, Northern Cheyenne and Arapaho people against the 7th Cavalry Regiment of the United States Army.

1885   Grover Cleveland is elected as the 22nd President.

1890   National American Woman Suffrage Association (NAWSA) is founded, with Elizabeth Cady Stanton as president.

1890   Monopolies are banned as the Sherman Antitrust Act is passed

1890   The Battle of Wounded Knee is the final battle found in the Indian Wars.

1892   Ellis Island is designated as the official immigration center of the United States. All immigrants pass through here

1893   Grover Cleveland is elected the 24th president making him the only president to serve two nonconsecutive terms.

1896   The Supreme Court upholds "separate but equal by stating that segregation is constitutional in Plessy v. Ferguson. Jim Crow laws are reinforced by this move and continue to oppress blacks.

1897   William McKinley is elected as the 25th president

1898   USS Maine is blown up in Havana Cuba. US declares War on Spain beginning the Spanish-American War:

1899   American Samoa is given to the U.S. through a treaty with Germany and Britain.

1900   Thousands are killed when the Galveston hurricane hits Texas.

1901   Theodore Roosevelt is inaugurated as President after the death of McKinley.

1903   U.S. acquires Panama Canal Zone (treaty signed Nov. 17).

1903   Wright brothers make the first controlled, sustained flight in heavier-than-air aircraft at Kitty Hawk, N.C. (Dec. 17).

1905   Theodore Roosevelt's second inauguration (March 4).

1909   William Howard Taft is inaugurated as the 27th president (March 4). Mrs. Taft has 80 Japanese cherry trees planted along the banks of the Potomac River.

1913   Woodrow Wilson is inaugurated as the 28th president (March 4). Seventeenth Amendment to the Constitution is ratified, providing for the direct election of U.S. senators by popular vote rather than by the state legislatures (April 8).

1914-1918   World War I: U.S. enters World War I

1914   Arch Duke Ferdinand's assassination in Sarajevo begins war

1914   Panama Canal opens

1917   Wilson's is reelected.

1919   League of Nations is created. This is a precursor to the United Nations. The US is not a member. The Treaty of Versailles is signed which forces Germany to take responsibility for the war and to make reparations. This treaty later led to the attitude of nationalism that helped propel Hitler into power.

1919   Prohibition. Alcohol is banned with the Eighteenth Amendment. Later it is overturned with the Twenty-First Amendment in 1933.

1920   Nineteenth Amendment ratified prohibits each state and the federal government from denying any citizen the right to vote based on that citizen's sex.

1921   Warren G. Harding is inaugurated as the 29th president (March 4). He signs resolution declaring peace with Austria and Germany (July 2).

1923   Vice President Calvin Coolidge becomes president after Harding's death.

1925   The Scopes Monkey trial causes a national debate about the teaching of evolution in public schools.

1927   Charles Lindbergh makes the first solo nonstop transatlantic flight in his plane The Spirit of St. Louis

1929   Herbert Hoover is elected as the 31st president (March 4).

1929   The Great Depression begins with the Stock Market Crash.

1931   National anthem becomes: The Star-Spangled Banner

1932   Amelia Earhart flies across the Atlantic Ocean solo

1933   (FDR) Franklin Roosevelt is elected as the 32nd president he begins his promise of the New Deal to try to help with economic recovery from the Depression.

1935   Works Progress Administration is established (April 8). Social Security Act is passed (Aug. 14). Bureau of Investigation (established 1908) becomes the Federal Bureau of Investigation under J. Edgar Hoover

1937   FDR is reelected

1938   Fair Labor Standards Act is passed, setting the first minimum wage in the U.S. at 25 cents per hour (June 25).

1939-1945   World War II: At first the US declares that it is neutral. However the bombing at Pearl Harbor by the Japanese on December 7, 1941 forces the US to declare War on Japan. Germany and Italy declare war on the US. The US responds by declaring War. FDR is reelected for a third term in 1941 and again for a fourth term in 1945. D –Day at Normandy as Allies invade France. Germany surrenders. 1945 When FDR dies of a stroke in 1945 he is succeeded by his Vice President Harry Truman.

1945   The Atomic bomb is dropped on Hiroshima and Nagasaki Japan by the US. Japan surrenders.

1945   United Nations is established (Oct. 24).

1948   Marshal Plan is passed by Congress as part of post war recovery efforts in Europe

Soviets begin blockade of Berlin in the first major crisis of the cold war (June 24). In response, U.S. and Great Britain begin airlift of food and fuel to West Berlin (June 26).

1949   Truman is reelected as president. North Atlantic Treaty Organization (NATO) is formed.

1950-1953   Truman enters the Korean War without approval from Congress. Communism and Non-Communist forces class in South Korea Armistice agreement is signed.

1950-1975   The United States is involved in the Vietnam War which is another War with the conflict of communist ideas as the source. The United States had many protests against this war and young people who "dodged the draft" feeling it was an unjust war.

1951   Presidential term limits are set to two terms. This is the Twenty Second Amendment to the Constitution.

1952   Puerto Rico becomes a U.S. commonwealth (July 25).

1952   Hydrogen bomb is detonated in the Marshall Islands.

1953   Dwight Eisenhower is elected as the 34th president

1954   "The McCarthy Era" Sen. Joseph R. McCarthy publically accuses many known figures and military members of being Communist Sympathizers

1954   Brown v. Board of Education of Topeka, Kansas Declares that Racial Segregation is unconstitutional.

1957   **is a very important year to know:**

1957   President Eisenhower is forced to send Federal Troops to Little Rock Arkansas because of forced integration of public schools. Central High School in Arkansas is backed Governor Orval Faubus. And the students who were trying to integrate became known as the Little Rock Nine.

1957   Sputnik 1 was the first Earth-orbiting artificial satellite. It was launched into an elliptical low Earth orbit by the Soviet Union on 4 October 1957, and ignited the Space Race within the Cold War. Because of this the US began spending major funding on Science Programs in American public schools.

1958   Explorer I, first American satellite, is launched

1959   Alaska and Hawaii become states.

1961   Problems with Cuba lead to the U.S. cutting off diplomatic relations. Later the invasion known as the Bay of Pigs is a disaster.

1961   John F. Kennedy is elected as the 35th president

1962   U.S. astronaut John Glenn becomes the first man to orbit the Earth

1962   Cuban Missile Crisis: The Soviet Union secretly installs missels on Cuba resulting in President Kennedy calling for a a naval blockade of the island.

1963   "I Have a Dream" Dr. Martin Luther King, Jr., delivers his speech before a crowd of 200,000 during the civil rights march on Washington, DC (Aug. 28).

1963   President Kennedy is assassinated in Dallas, Texas Lyndon B. Johnson is inaugurated as president.

1964   The Civil Rights Act prohibiting discrimination based on race, color, religion, sex, and national origin by federal and state governments as well as some public places– is signed by Johnson.

1965   President Johnson signs the Voting Rights Act, which prohibits discriminatory voting practices

1966   Miranda Rights set because of court case Miranda v. Arizona and because of this the Fourteenth Amendment outlines due process rights.

1968   This year is covered in an excellent online video on Youtube.com Look for: 1968 The Year that Shaped a Generation.

Rev. Martin Luther King, Jr., is assassinated in Memphis, Tenn. Sen. Robert F. Kennedy is assassinated in Los Angeles, Calif.

1969   The United States NASA program lands on the moon and is watched on television by Americans as Walter Cronkite hosts the special Astronauts on the historic flight include: Neil Armstrong and Edwin (Buzz) Aldrin, Jr., Space Race Era ends as the US claims the moon in the name of Earth, not the United States.

1969   Richard Nixon is elected President

1970   Kent State University is in the news as National Guardsmen kill four students during a protest against the war

1971   The Twenty-Sixth Amendment to the Constitution is ratified, lowering the voting age from 21 to 18 (July 1).

1972   Watergate Scandal. Nixon covers up a break in at the Watergate Complex in Washington DC.

1973   Nixon is reelected

1973   Abortion is legalized in the first trimester by the Supreme Court. Roe v. Wade

1973   Scandals in the White House: Vice President Spiro T. Agnew resigns over charges of corruption and income tax evasion. Gerald Ford takes over as VP.

1974   President Nixon is impeached for abuse of power and obstruction of justice. He resigns and Gerald Ford becomes President who grants Nixon a full Presidential Pardon. (many people feel that Ford lost the next election because of this act.)

1977   Jimmy Carter is elected as the 39th President. Panama Canal makes the news again as control is turned over to Panama by President Carter.

1978   Camp David Accord is signed by Anwar Sadat and Israeli prime minister Menachem Begin ending 30-year conflict between Egypt and Israel. Jimmy Carter is instrumental in this.

1979   Three Mile Island nuclear reactor in Pennsylvania has a meltdown causing fear in surrounding states.

1979   Iranian Hostage Crisis: Iranian students storm U.S. embassy in Teheran and hold 66 people hostage 13 of the hostages are released

1981   Ronald Reagan is elected the 40th president Assassination attempt on President Reagan by John Hinckley, Jr.

1981   Sandra Day O'Connor is sworn in as the first woman Supreme Court justice

1982   Deadline for ratification of the Equal Rights Amendment to the Constitution passes without the necessary votes

1985   Reagan is reelected.

1986   Space shuttle Challenger explodes 73 seconds after liftoff, killing all seven crew members including teacher Christa Mc Auliffe

1987   In a speech in Berlin, President Reagan challenges Soviet leader Mikhail Gorbachev to "tear down this wall" and open Eastern Europe to political and economic reform Reagan and Gorbachev sign INF treaty, the first arms-control agreement to reduce the superpowers' nuclear weapons

1989   George H. W. Bush is elected as the 41st president

1990   Iraqi troops invade Kuwait,

1991   Operation "Desert Storm" Unite Nation's international military embargo against Iraq lead by the US. Persian Gulf War

1992   End of the Cold War as the Soviet Union Dissolves

Interesting contributions from around the world:

- China gunpowder and fireworks, compass, silk and ink.

- Egypt papyrus, Pyramids, Sports,

- India Tea, The number zero and the decimal system, caste system (A person is born into a caste and can't move up or down. Unlike the Class system in the US where people have more flexibility in status.)

- Greece: money, the steam engine, Democracy, and the Olympics

- Rome: created the first streets, roads, and aqueducts.

- Arabic culture developed Algebra

Types of Political Systems

The following are examples of political systems:

- Democracy Rule by majority

- Monarchy. Rule by monarch Tribal Structure where authority rests with the absolute ruler. Monarchies are one of the oldest political systems known.

- Republic. (rule by law) The first recorded republic was in India in the 6th century BC.

- Theocracy Rule by representative of God. Vatican City is an example of a Theocracy.

- Feudalism This system had a manor or property on which many poor families would live. The owner of the manor was called the Lord, and was run by serfs or peasants who worked the land as laborers or paid taxes. An example of this system can be found in stories like Robin Hood.

Note that the United States is both a Republic and a Democracy. This is created by the "checks and balances" of the United States. Three branches of government share power: The Legislative (Congress) The Executive (The President) and Judicial (The Supreme Court) This strategy is in place to protect against "majority rule," a philosophy discussed by John Stuart Mill. "Tyranny of the majority" is unconstitutional in the US, with several cases in the news that illustrate this unfairness. The most commonly known is segregation during the 1960s where the minority group, African Americans, was oppressed because of the voting practices in the South. A recent example is Proposition 8 in California which voted on the marriage rights of homosexuals. Since homosexuals are a minority, the vote had the same effect. It is considered by many to be unconstitutional.

Likewise the United Kingdom uses a **constitutional monarchy.** This system is a form of government in which a monarch acts as head of state. In addition there is a "blended" constitution which is guided by a parliamentary system which is governed by the elected Prime Minister.

Rights and Responsibilities of US Citizens

Citizens are legally required to serve in Jury Duty.

Citizens are legally required to register their children in school. Homeschooling is considered registering a child to receive education. All children are mandated to receive an education.

Citizens are expected to obey laws and also to pay taxes.

US Citizens are encouraged to participate in the government by voting. However it is not a legal responsibility to vote.

The Civil Rights Movement:

Although most teachers I work with are familiar with the Civil Rights Movement, some don't remember all the details. Also foreign teachers are often not very familiar with this era. So I am making this section very simple to understand. The most famous movement in US History is the Civil Rights movement. Lasting from about 1955 until 1968 it concerned the Rights of African Americans in the United States.

Prior to the Civil Rights movement there were two court rulings that had a major impact on the educational rights of African Americans in the United States. The first was Plessy vs Ferguson which happened many years earlier in 1896. (a way I help students remember this is Plessy is Messy. Plessy made a huge mess in the United States) This ruling is shocking to modern Americans because it ruled that African Americans were not allowed to eat in the same restaurants, go to the same schools and live in the same neighborhood as white people simply because of the color of their skin. It is a very sad part of American history that has hurt and oppressed many of our citizens. This ruling "upheld Segregation as legal."

Many years later the case Brown v. Board of Education of Topeka Kansas 1954 overturned Plessy v. Ferguson. The Supreme Court ruled that schools must be desegregated.

Although the laws were changing, people's attitudes were not, which led to some of the following moments in history.

Rosa Parks and the Montgomery Bus Boycott, 1955-1956. When Rosa Parks would not give up her seat on a bus so that a white man could sit down, she was arrested. This arrest sparked outrage among the African American community and others who were sympathetic to their fight.

Montgomery Alabama's buses were boycotted for 381 days until the full desegregation was mandated on the buses.

President Eisenhower federalizes the National Guard In Little Rock Arkansas to enforce desegregation at Central High School 1957

Lunch Counters at Woolworths stores were the scene of "sit-ins" during the 1960s. "Sit ins" were peaceful protests during which African Americans would refuse to leave the white section of the lunch counters until they were served. All were usually arrested. This form of protest is known as "Civil Disobedience" and was supported by Dr. Martin Luther King Jr. who felt man had a moral obligation to disobey an unjust law.

March on Washington, 1963 Dr. King delivers his famous "I Have a Dream" speech at the National Mall in Washington D.C.

1968 Dr. King is assassinated the day after giving his "Mountaintop" speech in Memphis Tennessee. Major riots break out in the United States.

Chapter 17

CLASSIC WRITERS, FINE ARTS AND MUSIC

Many of the questions in the Fine Arts section are things you may have learned in college or high school but have forgotten. Pay attention to your strengths and weaknesses in this area and brush up on the areas you don't remember well.

Classic Writers:

Playwrights:

Sophocles, Aeschylus and Euripides	known for Tragedy
Aristophanes, Plautus and Terence.	known for Comedy
William Shakespeare	Tragedy and Comedy

Known for Iambic pentameter and rhyming couplets. Romeo and Juliet, Macbeth, Hamlet and King Lear.

Novelists:

Charles Dickens   Great Expectations

Details: The story of the orphan Pip, writing about his life as he struggles with morality, poverty and growing up.

Theme: Poverty and social problems resulting from industrialization in England.

Mark Twain   Adventures of Tom Sawyer

Details: pen name for Samuel Langhorne Clemens. Usually stories about boys on the riverboats in Mississippi.

Theme: Writes with a sense of satire and considered one of the greatest humorists in his era. Often uses wry criticism of American culture and literature.

Herman Melville   Moby Dick

Details: The story takes place on a ship where the narrator is Ishmael and Captain Ahab is obsessed with hunting a great white whale.

Theme: It is a story about the struggle between the human world and the natural world.

Poets

The exam covers classic poets. The exam also attempts to foster an appreciation for diversity by examining poetry written by ethnic writers. When reading a poem it is important to pay attention to the descriptions and emotions in the poem. All poetry should be symbolic in some way. Also look for the title of the poem to give you a clue about the theme. Do not choose answers that talk about the imagery in the poem in a literal manner. For example a poem that talks about "*a hawk stalking its prey*" is not discussing the hunting habits of birds. It will be a symbolic description of a human condition. An easy way for you to get trapped on a question is to answer the question literally.

Emily Dickinson is a poet who is known for her symbolic imagery through use of similes and metaphors. Her poems are often short, use unconventional rhyming structures, lack punctuation and capitalization. Ex:

hope is the thing with feathers
that perches in the soul,
and sings the tune without the words,
and never stops at all.

John Keats is a influential romantic era poet who is known for his sensual imagery. He often writes odes. His most famous is "Ode on a Grecian Urn."

Maya Angelou is an African American poet writes about the black experience in the United States. She is known for her rhythmic and lyrical way of reading her poems. Her imagery often depicts strong, proud black women. Maya Angelou uses repetition and musicality in her poetry. Phenomenal Woman, And Still I Rise,

Naomi Shihab Nye is an Arab American poet of Palestinian descent. Her first book of poems, Different Ways to Pray explores the theme of similarities and differences in cultures around the world. She is known for her use of free verse and her use of strong imagery. As a Palestinian American she often writes of the experiences as young woman and the theme of struggles with survival.

Pablo Neruda is the pen name of Chilean born poet, Neftali Ricardo Reyes Basoalto. Neruda's poetry often has themes of highs and lows. He writes in a style that contrasts the optimism in life with the darker side of man. His book *Twenty Love Poems and a Song of Despair* reflects this in a romantic theme.

Claude McKay was a Jamaican American writer and poet who was well known during the Harlem Renaissance. His book of poetry entitled "Harlem Shadows" was a pioneering book during this era. He was considered militant by some but also described a conflict in emotions in how he felt about America. Although he was highly critical of American racism, he felt that the country itself could be the source of the power to change it.

Painting and Graphic Arts

This section usually helps the test takers improve the most. Many people are intimidated by this topic. People tend to forget much of the art learned in the CORE requirements at college. It is important to not get intimidated in this section. Many times when I teach this section in class I'll discuss a picture that is on the exam. I'll say this:

Does anyone remember seeing the woodcut drawing of the Japanese woman with the little boy and the bird?

> A.   *Oh yes the bird! I remember that picture!*

It is odd to me that students remember the picture and especially the bird. Yet when asked about the question on the exam, most students think the answer must be more complicated. The question asks something like:

Why do you think the artist arranged the images diagonally?

> A.   To draw the viewers attention to the bird.
>
> B.   To demonstrate the difference in status between the woman and the boy
>
> C.   To give a sense of the artists perspective
>
> D.   To suggest a sense of parameter of the frame.

Most of the students pick B by mistake. They confuse the word "status" with "stature" and think it is about the difference in height. But status means a political or social difference. You wouldn't be able to tell that from a diagonal arrangement. It is curious to me that students remember the picture because of the bird but they don't think that is the answer. I'm sure many of you know exactly what picture I am talking about. The way to answer the art pictures is to rely only on what you see when you look at the picture. This is a section where "over-thinking" becomes a real problem. When you look at the piece of art, what do *you* see? Don't worry about remembering history or understanding the story behind the painting or picture. Some of the artists included on the exam are:

René Magritte is a Belgium artist. His *La Chambre d'Écoute* (The Listening Room) is a picture of a giant apple in a room. When you look at the picture the first thing that strikes you is the use of proportion. The apple is too big to be in the room.

Georgia O'Keefe is American Artist. *Cow Skull: Red White and Blue* and *Red Poppy* are two of her most well known paintings. Georgia O'Keefe paints using ordinary objects like flowers and skulls to suggest abstract meaning. Many of her paintings of flowers are considered to be erotic.

Andy Warhol is an American painter known for his style in media and Pop Art. *Tomato Soup Cans* and *Four Marilyns* are two of his most famous works. He rose to fame during the 1960s for his prints, films and paintings. His work is often considered a commentary on American consumerism. He is noted for his use of repetition and bright colors.

Marc Chagall was a Jewish French Artist who often used personal interpretation of his life as inspiration of his art. His painting *"Me and My Village"* is often used as an example of symbolism, cubism and surrealism.

Vincent van Gough was a Dutch post-impressionist painter. He suffered from mental illness and at one point famously cut off his own ear. His paintings are often of landscapes and are noted for the use of color and movement. The most famous of his works include *The Starry Night, Still Life: Vase with Twelve Sunflowers, and Café Terrace at Night.*

Edgar Degas was a French Painter most famous for his paintings of ballet dancers. He also did a sculpture called *Little Dancer of Fourteen Years.*

Pablo Picasso was a Spanish Painter. He is famous for his use of cubism and painting with different techniques. One of his most famous paintings is called *Guernica* which depicts in graphic detail the bombing of Guernica

Spain by Germany and Italy during the Spanish Civil War. This painting is considered an "anti-war" symbol. He is more famously known for his paintings in his "Blue Period" which depict poor looking subjects of men women and children. His painting *The Old Guitarist* is one of the most well known in this period.

Jackson Pollock is an American artist who is famous for his abstract impressionism. His unique style of painting is what he is most known for. His works were often painted laid flat on the ground as he dribbled and flung paint at the canvas. His pieces were often known by number titles. *Number 1* and *Number 5* etc.

Michelangelo is an Italian Renaissance painter and sculpture who is known for many pieces including *The Sistine Chapel* and the statue of *David*. These works were commissioned by the Pope and Catholic Church. His works are often biblical in nature and are flowing and lush.

Leonardo da Vinci was an Italian painter. He is famous however for his inventions, science, math and works of anatomy. He is often considered a "Renaissance man" a term that means a man who studies many different disciplines. His most famous work is the *Mona Lisa*, a painting that still today is considered a mystery. Like Michelangelo he often painting biblical inspirations. The most famous of these is *The Last Supper*.

On the exam there will be other artists who are not as well known. The important approach in looking at the picture is to keep it as simple as possible. What do *you* see when you look at the picture? Why do you think the artists created the image? What kinds of moods are present in the picture? Pictures that show dancers for example are often talking about movement. How are dancers positioned? If they are up in the air then the answers probably reflect the idea of flight, air, and light. If they are curled up on the ground then the answers are probably about sadness and earth. If questions are asking you to describe the mood or tone of the painting you should look at the posture of the people in the paintings. How do they relate to the other images? Trust your own eyes in this section and keep it as simple as possible.

Music

(source: http://www.classicalworks.com/html/glossary.html)

Clef note: A symbol indicating the pitch to be played. Usually a G clef or a Bass clef, those scrolling shapes at the front of the staff.

Harmony—Pleasing combination of two or three tones played together in the background while a melody is being played. Harmony also refers to the study of chord progressions.

Key—System of notes or tones based on and named after the key note.

Measure—The unit of measure where the beats on the lines of the staff are divided up into two, three, four beats to a measure.

Melody—the sequence of single tones in a song, as opposed to Harmony or rhythm.

Movement—A separate section of a larger composition.

Pitch—The frequency of a note determining how high or low it sounds.

Refrain—A repeating phrase that is played at the end of each verse in the song.

Rhythm—The element of music pertaining to time, played as a grouping of notes into accented and unaccented beats.

Scale—Successive notes of a key or mode either ascending or descending. the song.

Staff—Made up of five horizontal parallel lines and the spaces between them on which musical notation is written.

Tempo—Indicating speed.

Tune–A rhythmic succession of musical tones, a melody for **instruments and voices.**

Time Signature–A numeric symbol in sheet music determining the number of beats to a measure.

Whole note–A whole note is equal to 2 half notes, 4 quarter notes, 8 eighth notes, etc.

Types of Instruments and their sounds

(source http://exhibits.pacsci.org/music/Instruments.html)

Strings Stringed instruments are characterized by having (you guessed it!) strings.

How the sounds are made

Vibrating strings provide the sound in stringed instruments. The player makes the strings vibrate in one of several ways:

Plucking, as with the harp, guitar, and mandolin

Bowing, as with the violin family Note that instruments in the violin family can be played two ways: bowing and plucking.

Hitting, as with the hammered dulcimer and piano

Violin family: violin, viola cello, bass, Guitar, lyre, koto, harp, lute banjo.

Woodwinds At one time, most woodwinds were made of wood; hence the name. The easiest way to characterize them now is as wind instruments (that is, you blow into them) which aren't played by buzzing your lips together.

How the sounds are made

Most woodwind instruments are tubes. The sound comes from a vibrating column of air inside the tube. The player makes this column of air vibrate in one of several ways:

By blowing across an edge, as in the flute, recorder, whistle, and root beer bottle

By blowing between a reed and a fixed surface, as in the clarinet and saxophone

By blowing between two reeds, as in the oboe, bassoon, and bagpipes

Flute, clarinet, saxophone, oboe, bassoon,

Brass Most brass instruments from the Western European tradition really are made of brass, but there are large numbers of brass-type instruments which are made of wood, horn, shell, or other materials.

How the sounds are made

As with woodwinds, the sound comes from a vibrating column of air inside the tube of the instrument. The air column vibrates in resonance with the vibrating lips of the player, who presses her or his lips together in the mouthpiece and forces air out between them, making a "raspberry" or "Bronx cheer" sound.

Trumpet, trombone, French horn, tuba, bugle

Percussion Percussion instruments include just about anything you can whack with a stick.

How the sounds are made

In percussion instruments the sound source is a vibrating membrane (these instruments are called *membranophones*) or vibrating piece of solid material (these are *ideophones*). The percussionist normally causes these materials to vibrate by hitting them (hence the name *percussion*), but many percussion instruments are played by shaking, rubbing, or any other way of causing vibrations.

Drums, xylophone, maracas, cymbals, gong

Chapter 18

CST MULTI SUBJECT ESSAY

The Multi Subject Essay is a very simple essay to write. The strategies listed below work very well. When I used these on the essay I received a 300 on the essay and it took me about 10 minutes to write the essay. I love the support that these strategies offer because they are easy to master and they work. As always, keep in mind that the essay is only worth about 10% of the overall test score. ***The essay will not "save" you from failing the exam.*** This is very important to remember. Use your time wisely.

Your Goal: To write a simple three paragraph essay in about 30 minutes. A 220 is a passing score on the essay.

Structure of the essay:

1. The first paragraph will identify weaknesses in an oral reading prompt. There should be 2-3 examples of Word Analysis issues. For each one of these examples there should be several examples of the same type of issue.

2. The Second Paragraph will discuss how the student's reading ability affected by the difficulties in the first paragraph. What can a teacher do to help?

3. The Third Paragraph will discuss the interview between the student and the Teacher. It will explore the difficulties the student has in his reading comprehension. Generally this will focus on literal and inferential comprehension. It will focus on whether or not the student understands the story they have just read in the session.

What you will need to write the essay:

*   **Proper terminology**
*   **The ability to recognize patterns in the essay prompt.**
*   **An understanding of phonemic awareness and the way students learn to read.**
*   **Understanding the importance of pacing and fluency and automaticity.**
*   **Understanding orthographic awareness.**
*   **Understanding of the difference between inferential and literal comprehension.**
*   **Good grammar, punctuation and organization skills.**

Some of these terms seem intimidating but they are easy to understand and to use on the essay. Don't worry.

Let's begin!

How do we learn to read?

In order to understand the goal of the essay question, we first need to think about how we learn to read.

We learn to read by using phonics, using our speaking vocabulary when we don't recognize a word and using context to help us figure out what unfamiliar words might be. Phonemic awareness is the ability to recognize that a spoken word is composed of a sequence of individual sounds (phonemes). This skill is about seeing the words based on "sound clusters" and contributes to the ability to decode new words with similar sound clusters. Phonemic awareness helps with both reading and spelling. This awareness is learned over time as students practice reading and writing.

Young children also learn to read by **speaking**. As a child reads the words on the page they begin to "fill in" unfamiliar words with their speaking vocabulary. Most people read in this manner. We are able to almost "jump ahead" in reading if we understand the context of a sentence. For example if I write:

I went into the _____and opened the _____and took out the milk.

A typical adult English speaking reader would probably be able to fill in the blanks. *"I went into the kitchen and opened the refrigerator and took out the milk."*

This skill is a very important tool in reading. When a child reads a word they don't understand sometimes they will try to sound out the word. Most times however, and *especially in the examples given on the exam*, the reader will substitute words they do know for the word they do not understand. Sometimes the student substitutes a word that is a correct "context" substitution:

For example

I walked the dog to the store and bought a new leash.

Is read as

I walked the dog to the store and got a new leash.

This kind of error can be a good example of the student trying to maintain his pace while reading. The sentence still makes sense the way the student read it. Yet this kind of substitution is obviously wrong because it is not what is written on the page. You want to notice a pattern in the student's errors. (Just remember we *never* call them errors in the essay!)

Word substitution is a typical Word Analysis issue that is used on the CST Multi Subject Essay. Pay attention to how the substitution is happening. Is the student using contextually correct words, or just wrong words?

For example

I walked the dog to the store and bought a new leash.

Is read as

I want the dog to the store and bring a now lash.

This is a different kind of error. If a child is reading like this we can see that he is going to have difficulty following along and understanding the actual story.

Most word substitution errors I have seen on the exam are pronoun substitutions. Your, our, he, she etc.

There are also errors with proper word usage that includes suffix endings, conventions, syntax and context. Errors with tenses are rare but are easily identifiable if they do occur.

Always remember to look for a pattern, not just a one-time mistake. Anyone can make a one-time mistake. You should see a pattern of similar mistakes. (Remember we *never* call them mistakes on the essay.)

What you will need to do for Word Analysis:

- ➢ Read the excerpt as it is written and then again with the mistakes. This way you keep in mind what the reader is reading.
- ➢ Find a type of mistake that the reader makes two or three times.
- ➢ Look to see if he or she says a word with a similar structure correctly elsewhere in the passage.
- ➢ **Typical Types of Word Analysis issues include:**

  - ➢ *Consonant digraph, cluster or blend*
  - ➢ *Pronoun substitution or Word Substitution*
  - ➢ *Word endings, Suffix ending, Base words*
  - ➢ *Fluency, Pacing, Automaticity, Phonemic Awareness, Orthographic Awareness,*

Common Mistakes that Teachers Make on this section:

Not using the proper terminology:

If the child makes a mistake with suffix endings, you need to write "suffix endings" not word endings. There is a difference between a "suffix" and the end of a word. For example: "walked" read as "walks" is a suffix ending. The word "vocabulary" read as "vocabulaby" is not a suffix ending. It is a word ending. Points will be taken off for this error.

Using negative terminology. You should NOT say words and phrases listed below:

- *Makes mistakes or errors*
- *Has a problem with*
- *Can't, doesn't, won't*
- *Should have*

You should say:

- *Demonstrates difficulty*
- *Needs support in the area of . . .*
- *Struggles with*

Only looking for errors:

A common mistake I see with teachers who have repeatedly taken the exam is that the teacher only sees the errors on the page and not the patterns. Many of the essay prompts deliberately will have a student read a phonic sound correctly elsewhere in the passage. If the teacher doesn't notice this was read correctly, the essay will have points taken off. This is because you are expected to assess the entire reading record and interview, not just look for errors. We will discuss this more later.

Not properly documenting the difficulty:

The proper way to document an error is to write the word that was **read** and also the word that was **written**. Some teachers only write what the student said. For example: ***Timmy read got by mistake.*** You need to use quotation marks. For example: ***Timmy read "got" when the written word was "bought."*** This is clearly indicating what was said and what was written.

Only writing about one area of need:

Even though the prompt asks you to identify one area of need in Word Analysis and one in Reading Comprehension, you should write at least two or three examples in the first paragraph and try to discuss two areas in the Reading Comprehension paragraph.

Writing from a Teacher Centered Perspective

Many teachers get into the habit of writing from a "teacher centered" perspective. It is understandable that a teacher would do this because it seems as though you are being asked to defend yourself as a teacher. This essay should be written as a form of documentation and focus on the student in a positive and supportive way. It should not use judging words and it should demonstrate a desire to assist this student. You should also not say "I" in the essay.

Here is an example of a BAD Paragraph: WRONG!

The record of Timmy's oral reading record shows he has problems with consonant clusters. He says bringed and teached by mistake. As I read through the essay I found a lot of mistakes and problems. He also messed up by reading the wrong tense instead of the right one.

What is wrong here? Well first of all it says "problems, mistakes and messed up." Second it is teacher centered and talks about the teacher's observations and uses the word "I." Finally it isn't documented correctly. Although the teacher writes that he says "bringed and teached" it doesn't show what was actually written. Documentation must be clear and use quotation marks. In addition it doesn't show a clear assessment of both strengths and weaknesses that will help develop a strategy for assisting the student.

Word Identification Strategies:

1. Knowledge of phonics (phonemic awareness)–recognition of words through grapheme-phoneme association. The typical essay will include one of the following types of phonics issues:

- Decoding consonant clusters: pa**tch** is read as path, bu**nch** is read as bush
- Decoding consonant diagraphs (two letters pronounced as one sound): wa**sh**ed, mo**th**er
- Decoding two letter consonant blends: **sw**eet, **br**eak.

The above word analysis difficulties are usually one of the mistakes that are typically made by a reader.

You also want to be sure that once you have identified the error you will skim through the paragraph to see if the student is correctly identifying the same type of phonics elsewhere. For example: Look at the two "errors" that the student, Timmy, makes when reading this aloud:

> John was getting ready to go swimming at the beach. He
>
> ***bringed***
> thought about meeting his friends. He had <u>brought</u> a tennis set and wanted to play along the shore. His father had
>
> ***teached***
> <u>taught</u> him a secret move that he was sure would help him win the game.

Many teachers will notice the words "brought" and "taught" were read incorrectly. And so they will write: *"Timmy has a problem with consonant clusters. He can't read the "ght" word ending correctly."*

And they **gotcha!** If we skim through the reading we will notice that Timmy correctly decodes the word "thought."

This is a very significant issue in this student's reading. This has to do with **"orthographic awareness."** Now don't get worried about understanding all the details of "orthographic awareness." For the purposes of the essay we're going to simplify it. If you want to do research on it you can use the internet. However it is not necessary to know that much information in order to use it in the essay.

Basically orthographic awareness is the way readers use the ability to read one word correctly, to help them decode the other words in the passage. In Timmy's case, the fact that he was able to read the word "thought" means that he should have been able to use that skill to decode the words "brought" and "taught."

Remember, this is about finding the patterns. We would *never* write that Timmy "should have" been able to use that skill to help decode the words in the essay. Instead we would something like this:

The record of Timmy's oral reading demonstrates a need of support in the area of consonant clusters. Although he correctly reads the word "thought" he struggles elsewhere. He reads "bringed" when the written word is "brought" and he reads "teached" when the written word is "taught." A teacher of such a student would work on helping Timmy to develop his orthographic awareness and phonemic awareness.

In this case we also have another error; this error is one about convention. This would be an error in word structure. We notice that Timmy is not using the appropriate grammar tense. You always want to look for patterns of errors. *(remember we never call them errors on the exam.)* Dropping the "ly" ending from adverbs is another common error I have seen on the exam.

The final issue would be the use of automaticity. *(Don't try saying this three times fast because you will get tongue tied!)*

Auto-ma-ti-city. Don't be intimidated by the word if you don't know it. You can research it on the internet if you want to know more about it. But for the purposes of the essay we are going to keep it simple.

Automaticity is simply the way we all learn to read in an "automatic" way. When a child is a new reader they might read each word, one word at a time. But as a child improves in reading, his or her speed and accuracy should also improve. The same way we do not sound out words letter by letter, we also can read entire chunks of sentences rather than the sentence word by word. This has to do with pacing and fluency in a reading excerpt. If a child reads too slowly he needs to improve his pacing and automaticity. If the child reads too quickly he might need to improve his pacing and fluency. Fluency means understanding what we are reading as we are reading it. Pacing is how fast or slow we are reading.

The Second Paragraph

The second paragraph should be a short summary of what areas of support you feel would benefit the student. We write these a simple three or four line paragraphs. Keep it short. This paragraph connects the way the student struggles with word analysis to how it is going to interfere with his Reading Comprehension. Don't try to make a big deal out of this paragraph. Nearly every essay my students have written had the same type of second paragraph. Just pay attention to the differences in the patterns you have seen.

Ways to Help the Child Improve their Reading:

- Work on developing automaticity
- Encouraging use of orthographic awareness
- Helping the child with their fluency and pacing
- Developing stronger phonemic awareness
- Working with the student to activate prior knowledge and word recognition skills.

Examples:

- *A teacher of such a student would work on developing his automaticity. It would also be helpful to work with Timmy in using orthographic knowledge to identify and decode familiar words.*

> • *A teacher of such a student would work with Timmy on his phonemic awareness and fluency in reading. It would also be helpful to encourage the use or orthographic awareness and automaticity. This would take the focus off processing the sentence word by word and move towards improved reading comprehension.*

Although the vocabulary in this section is a little scary, don't be intimidated by it. They are just tools in your essay that will support your argument. You are only briefly mentioning them. You don't have to do anything more than use it in a sentence once in the essay. Just practice writing these kinds of sentences so on the day of the exam you will be prepared with the format. Trust me; you don't want to stumble on these sentences. They need to be written clearly and with ease so that it seems like you know what you are talking about. Practice, Practice, Practice.

The Third Paragraph: The Interview Section

Reading Comprehension

- Literal Comprehension–understanding the literal meaning of the text. This includes answers to questions that are led by the following words:

  - Who
  - Where

  - What
  - When

- Inferential Comprehension–understanding a message the text conveys using clues. These include the answers to the following types of questions:

  - What is the story about?
  - Why do you think this happened?
  - Why do you think the character acted that way?

Teachers often are confused by this section because there is a difference between a reader not understanding something that they have read correctly and not understanding something that they have read incorrectly. Let's look at the previous excerpt that Timmy read:

> John was getting ready to go swimming at the beach. He
> **_bringed_**
> thought about meeting his friends. He had <u>brought</u> a tennis
> set and wanted to play along the shore. His father had
> **_teached_**
> <u>taught</u> him a secret move that he was sure would help him
> win the game.

In this case we notice that Timmy has made some errors in reading *(Just remember we never call them errors in the essay.)* However it shouldn't interfere with his reading comprehension because he simply read the wrong tense and pronounced the word incorrectly. In this case it seems as though he still understands the details. He knows they were going to the beach; that he was meeting his friends; that John brought a tennis set and that his father had taught him a secret move. Let's look at some typical interview questions. The first set will be examples of **literal comprehension** questions:

Teacher: *What did John bring to the beach with him?*

Timmy: *He brought a tennis set with him.*

Teacher: *Where were they going to play tennis?*

Timmy: *Along the shore.*

In each case Timmy simply has to remember what he read in the passage and repeat the information. This is a literal comprehension type of interview. Let's look at some examples of **inferential comprehension** questions:

Teacher: *Who do you think John was going to play tennis with?*

Timmy: *He was going to play tennis with his friends.*

Teacher: *When was John going to the beach?*

Timmy: *He was going soon; he was getting ready to go with his dad.*

In each of these questions Timmy had to use clues from the story to figure out the answer to the question. It doesn't state clearly that he was going to play tennis with his friends. But we can deduce that this is what is happening. Additionally it doesn't say when exactly he was going to the beach but it gives clues that he was "getting ready" which Timmy correctly picked up on. If the student has to "figure out the answer" it is an inferential question.

This seems simple enough. However, in this excerpt Timmy didn't make any mistakes in reading that would effect his reading comprehension. On the exam the student will always make mistakes when he or she is reading. *(Just remember we never call them mistakes when we write the essay)* So let's look at an excerpt that has different kinds of mistakes:

really   **bench**

John was getting <u>ready</u> to go swimming at the <u>beach</u>. He

bringed

thought about meeting his friends. He had <u>brought</u> a tennis

shoe

set and wanted to play along the <u>shore</u>. His father had

teached   **more**

<u>taught</u> him a secret <u>move</u> that he was sure would help him win the game.

What is going to happen now? Well first of all when he's reading he doesn't read the word beach correctly. So Timmy is not going to understand that they are going to the beach. He also doesn't understand that he is playing on the shore because he reads this as **shoe**. This is where many teachers make mistakes and get trapped by the way they wrote the exam.

If Timmy doesn't read the word "beach" correctly and the teacher asks him the same questions he is not going to be able to answer them. Let's take a look:

Teacher: *What did John bring to the beach with him?*

Timmy: *I think he brought a shoe.*

Teacher: *Where were they going to play tennis?*

Timmy: *They were going to play tennis with his friends, at the playground I think.*

As you can see his reading comprehension is hurt by the fact that he doesn't understand what he is reading. It is important in your essay to make this distinction.

Let me say that again:

It is important in your essay to make this distinction.

It is not the same thing as literal comprehension if the reader doesn't understand what he just read because he didn't read it correctly. Many teachers would write that Timmy has poor literal reading comprehension. But we cannot deduce this from the errors he has made. Literal comprehension refers to going back to what you just read and remembering details. How can Timmy do that correctly if he just read it wrong? Instead we want to write something like this:

These difficulties have an effect on Timmy's literal comprehension skills because he did not correctly read the words on the page. Because of this it has a negative impact on his ability to recall details from the story. It also effects his inferential comprehension as he struggles with his fluency.

What we want to say is that it effects or has an impact on the literal comprehension skills. We do not want to say that Timmy has poor reading comprehension skills. It must be worded the way it is in the above excerpt. This way we are showing the exam grader that we made the distinction between the two issues.

If Timmy reads it correctly and still doesn't understand a literal question then we would write that he has difficulty with literal comprehension, but most of the time on the essay I do not see this kind of mistake. Instead I always see an error in the reading section that are later asked about in the interview. We will look at two examples of this in our practice essays at the end of this chapter.

Finally the inferential questions are usually pretty easy to identify. Just remember inferential questions require the student to use clues, emotions and behaviors of characters in the story to figure out the meaning. Usually the "moral of the story" is asked as an inferential comprehension question. Did the child understand the "point" of the story.

Now let's look at some practice essays!

Carl, whose only language is English, reads aloud a passage from an unfamiliar story. Printed below is an excerpt from the teacher's record of Carl's oral reading performance. *Partial word and sight word mistakes* are indicated.

---

looks   **them**
When Karen looked for her brother's birthday card, she couldn't find it anywhere. She

sershed   **her**   **their**
and her mother searched all over the house–in Karen's room, the living room and even

on   **kishen**
in the drawers under the kitchen sink. But no card was found. Now it was too late to

that   **thirteen**
buy another card, since the party was going to start in about thirty minutes. Karen

fustation   **Let   your**
began to cry in frustration. Her Mom then said, "I have a great idea! Let's make our own

claimed   **it   don't**
birthday card for Billy." Karen explained, "How can we do that? I only know how to buy

and   **quietly   sershed**
birthday cards at a store, not make them." But Karen and her mother quickly searched

or   **coloring   crayers   glistens**
and found what was needed– scissors, colored paper, glue, crayons and some glitter

be   over   she
from Karen's bead making kit. In about ten minutes, they created a beautiful birthday

wide   her   would
card. Smiling widely, Karen said, "This is the best card I could ever give anyone!"

What kind of patterns do we see in this excerpt? Well to begin we see that Carl has difficulty with consonant clusters. He mispronounces the sounds in the words: searched, kitchen, and frustration. The rch, tch, and str phonics sounds are all considered consonant clusters. This stands out right from the beginning. But we need to go back and see if Carl is able to read consonant clusters elsewhere. He does! Throughout the passage he correctly reads the word "birthday." The "rth" sound in birthday is also a consonant cluster.

We also notice that Carl continually uses word substitution with "pronouns." He says "your" instead of "our" and "she" instead of "they." Now we need to go back to see if he reads pronouns correctly in the passage. He does! He reads the words "her" and "she" several times correctly in the passage. Now we have two word analysis issues to write about.

Next let's take a look at his interview:

After reading the passage aloud, Carl rereads it silently. Then the teacher asks him some questions about the passage. Printed below is a transcript of their conversation.

Teacher: What is this story about?

Carl: It's about a girl who lost her brother's birthday card.

Teacher: Why was this such a big problem?

Carl: I think she didn't have enough money to buy another one.

Teacher: So what did Karen do?

Carl: She got her mother to make a card with stuff from around her house.

Teacher: Do you remember what material was used from something of Karen's?

Carl: Not really. Maybe from one of her old birthday cards that she saved.

Teacher: Why do you think Karen was so happy with the new birthday card for her brother?

Carl: She was just happy that she had card to give him so she wouldn't be embarrassed at the party.

Let's consider the issues here:

We see examples of both inferential and literal comprehension questions. Asking Carl, "Why do you think Karen was so happy . . . ." is an example of a "moral" or "point" of the story. This is an inferential question. Asking Carl, "Do you remember what material was used from something of Karen's?" is a literal question. However we need to be sure that Carl is not making reading errors on these important details. If he reads the part that contains these details we could say he has difficulty with literal comprehension. If he doesn't we need to say his word analysis difficulties are contributing to his literal comprehension issues.

Let's take a look: Carl reads–

               quietly   sershed or
But Karen and her mother quickly searched and found what was needed–

       coloring   crayers   glistens   be
scissors, colored paper, glue, crayons and some glitter from Karen's bead making kit

      over   she
In about ten minutes, they created a beautiful birthday card.

As we can see, Carl doesn't read the materials correctly. Therefore when he is asked to remember what materials Karen used, he cannot. This is a different kind of problem. To work with this student we will need to work on his Word Analysis skills.

There is another interesting issue with Carl. This has to do with his prior knowledge. As I stated in the beginning of this chapter, most young children learn to read by using their speaking language. The essay exam always points out that the reader is a native English speaker who is reading a passage aloud for the first time. Then the child reads it silently again before answering the questions. Now what is interesting to me about Carl here is that he should have been able to decode the materials used in the excerpt above. At the very least he should have decoded the word "crayers" properly because most students use crayons when they are in school. This goes back to context clues and comprehension. Most teachers who write the essays don't pay attention to these kinds of issues. Train your brain to look for them. You do not need to write about them but they will guide you in understanding what the essay exam is about.

Now Let's Write the Essay:

Examinee Task

Using your knowledge of **word identification strategies** (e.g., use of word structure, use of context clues, identification of sight words) and **reading comprehension** (e.g., literal comprehension, engagement in schema, self-monitoring) write and essay in which you:

- Identify one of Carl's needs in using **word identification strategies**, and explain how the information shown above supports your conclusion, citing specific examples: and

- Identify one of Carl's needs relating to **reading comprehension**, and explain how the information shown above supports your conclusion, citing specific examples.

Example A:

The record of Carl's reading demonstrates he has difficulty with phonemic awareness. Although he consistently reads the consonant cluster in the word "birthday" he needs support with this skill. He twice reads "sershed" when the written word is "searched." He reads "kishen" when the written word is "kitchen" and he reads "fustation" when written word is "frustration." He also demonstrates a need in the area of pronouns and context. Although he reads the word "her" and "she" accurately throughout the text, he incorrectly substitutes the pronouns "she" for "they," "them" for "it" and "your" for "our." A teacher of such a student would work on developing his automaticity and orthographic awareness to help with decoding words. It is also important for Carl to work on pacing and fluency so that he is reading the words on the page rather than simple substitutions.

The consequence of the above difficulties has an impact on Carl's reading comprehension skills. Because he is not reading the words on the page it impacts his literal comprehension skills. For example when asked to recall the materials used to make the card, Carl states that he didn't know what was used, perhaps some old birthday cards. Carl doesn't accurately decode the words that indicate craft items were used. This in turn also affects his inferential comprehension. Although Carl understood the basic concept of the missing birthday card, he failed to pick up clues that indicated the reasons for Karen's frustration was that there was not enough time to buy another card. He also misses the point of the story and thinks Karen is worried about being embarrassed rather than the idea that she is proud of making this card. It is important for Carl to work on pacing and fluency so that he is reading the words on the page rather than simple substitutions. By developing these skills and his word analysis skills Carl will also improve his reading comprehension.

Notice the wording, the examples and the supportive suggestions throughout the essay. This is something you want to do in your own essay. Let's look at another example written by a student in my class:

Example B:

The record of Carl's reading demonstrates he has difficulty with consonant clusters. Although he correctly decodes the word "birthday" several times throughout the section, elsewhere he struggles. For example he twice reads "sershed" when the written word is "searched"; he reads "kishen" when the written word is "kitchen" and he reads "fustation" when the written word is "frustration." In addition Carl shows a need of support in the area of suffix endings. He correctly identifies suffixes such as "ed" and "ly" throughout the passage. However in other places he struggles. For example he reads "looks" when the written word was "looked"; he reads "wide" when the written word was "widely".

A teacher of such a student would work on developing his automaticity and orthographic awareness to help him decode familiar word. In addition the teacher would support the student in encouraging his phonemic awareness.

Because of Carl's difficulty, he suffers in his reading comprehension. Although he understands the basic concept of the story that Karen doesn't have a birthday card for her brother, he struggles in other areas such as literal and inferential comprehension. For example when asked in the oral transcript if he remembered what materials were used to make Karen's birthday card, he said "not really". He guessed that it was one of her old birthday cards that she had saved because he did not accurately read the words in the story. In addition when asked why he thought Karen was happy with her new birthday card he replied "She was happy that she had a card to give him so she wouldn't be embarrassed. The passage stated that Karen was happy because she used "special" materials to make the card for her brother. It seems that Carl needs support in pacing. He read through the passage so quickly that he missed the point of why Karen was so happy. By developing these skills and his word analysis skills Carl will also improve his reading comprehension.

Let's try another Example:

In this next example be sure to look for the word substitutions. David will replace the words with other words that seem contextually correct. Then as his reading continues he gets more and more confused about what he is saying. Whenever you see something like this you want to be sure to always mention orthographic awareness, automaticity and pacing and fluency in the second paragraph.

Let's take a look:

David, whose only language is English, reads aloud a passage from an unfamiliar story. Printed below is an excerpt from the teacher's record of David's oral reading performance. Partial word and sight word mistakes are indicated.

He

Sally was so excited to finally put on her new, black, shiny shoes. Her mother had been

over   in the

promising that she could wear them on the next nice day. But today it rained all morning

and the ground was all wet and muddy. "I'm sorry that you can't bring your

could

shoes outside, dear, but you can wear them inside all day long if you want." Sally kept

upstair   his

staring down at her feet, even as she went upstairs to her room. But while her mother

could not   off

was busy fixing lunch, Sally just couldn't help herself. She raced out the door and

skip   notices

skipped down the street. After a few minutes, she ran back inside. Then she noticed

coverted   tick   Sally

that both shoes were scratched and covered with thick, brown mud. When Sally's

away   the

mother saw this, she told Sally to take off her shoes. "Now you have ruined your new

as   cry

shoes. They will never look so as nice." Sally started crying and learned an important

this

lesson *that* day.

After reading the passage aloud, David reads it silently. Then the teacher asks him some question about the passage. Printed below is a transcript of their conversation.

Teacher: What is this story about?

David: It's about a girl who got new shoes.

Teacher: What kind of shoes were they?

David: They were just regular shoes that she liked.

Teacher: Why did Sally's mother not allow her to go outside?

David: It was raining hard.

Teacher: What lesson do you think Sally learned at the end of the story?

David: Maybe that you can have more fun inside than if you were outdoors, especially if it's raining out.

Examinee Task

Using your knowledge of **word identification strategies** (e.g., use of word structure, use of context clues, identification of sight words) and **reading comprehension** (e.g., literal comprehension, engagement in schema, self-monitoring) write an essay in which you:

Identify one of David's needs in using **word identification strategies**, and explain how the information shown above supports your conclusion, citing specific examples: and

Identify one of David's needs relating to **reading comprehension**, and explain how the information shown above supports your conclusion, citing specific examples.

So what is going on?

In this exam question we can see that David has issues with suffix endings, word substitution, pronouns and convention. Convention means how a word is supposed to be used in English. Let's take a look at the sample essay.

The record of David's oral reading demonstrates a need of support in the area of word suffixes. Although he correctly decodes the words "staring" "scratched" and "raced," elsewhere he struggles. He reads "cry" when the word written is "crying"; he reads "skip" when the word written is "skipped" and he reads "notices" when the word written is "noticed." Additionally David demonstrates difficulty with pronouns. Although he correctly reads the words "she" and "her" throughout the passage he substitutes other pronouns, for example he reads "He" when the word written is "her"; he reads "his" when the written word was "her" and "the" when the written word is "your".

A teacher of such a student would work on developing his phonemic and orthographic awareness to help him decode words. Additionally it is important to focus on David's word substitution. Throughout the passage he substitutes contextually correct words that do not reflect the word written.

Because of the above difficulties David struggles with his reading comprehension. He is unable to correctly pick up context clues that would help him with his inferential comprehension. For example he misses the point that the shoes are special because of the emotions and reactions attributed to Sally and her mother: Sally was "so excited" to wear the shoes and she began crying when she saw they were ruined. In addition Sally's mother had been promising she could wear them. These clues indicate that the shoes were special. David misses the important details of the shoes being "covered with thick brown mud" because he reads instead, "coverted with tick brown mud." This affects his literal comprehension as well as he does not understand the words he reads. By working with David to focus on his pacing and automaticity a teacher can help him develop the fluency needed for accurate reading comprehension.

By following the patterns in the excerpts we can easily write a quick essay. The tricky part is to practice writing the essay so that when you go in to take the exam you have written an essay so much that it just flows out of your pencil. Even if you just copy these essays three times it will help develop the skills you need to pass the essay portion of the exam.

However it is important NOT to plagiarize any examples of essays you might find in any of the test prep books you use. If you do, you **will** fail the exam. The score on an essay that seems plagiarized is a **U, for unacceptable.** If the reader suspects you have plagiarized the essay but is uncertain, they will probably give you a **100**. And you will also fail the exam.

The essays in this prep book are examples of the word analysis and reading comprehension parts of the exam. They also will use symbols on the essay and give a key at the bottom for you to use to understand the meaning of the symbols. Most of the symbols involve repetition, pauses, attempts to sound out the words and self correction. Be sure to use these symbols to help you get a better sense of understanding how the student is reading as they go along.

The next few pages are Strategy reminders and Glossary terms that are important for you to know. Good luck on your essay!

Strategy:

> Read the excerpt as it is written and then again the way the student has read it.

> Look for phonics errors like consonant clusters, digraphs and blends. Double check to see a similar phoneme said correctly.

> Look for pronoun errors.

> Look for suffix errors.

> When seeing word substitution errors always look to see if the words are contextually correct or just simple substitution. *(Note: the difference will be important later on in the essay!)*

> Practice documenting the error correctly. Use quotation marks.

> Check out literal comprehension. Be sure that the student has read the words correctly. If not it is a different kind of problem.

> What kind, who, where etc are literal comprehension questions.

> Check out inferential comprehension. See if the student understood the "moral" or "point" of the story.

> ➤ **Why, why do you think etc. are inferential comprehension questions.**

Glossary:

automaticity: the ability to produce words or larger language units in a limited time interval (relates to fluency)

base word: a word to which a prefix or suffix may be added to form a new word (go + ing = going)

consonant blend: the joining of the sounds represented by two or more letters with minimal change in those sounds; consists of two or more consonants sounded together in such a way that each is heard (bl, gr, sp, etc.)

consonant digraph: consists of two consonants that together represent one sound (sh, ch, th, wh)

context clue: the information from the immediate textual setting that helps identify a word or word group

convention: accepted practice in written language **decode:** to analyze spoken or graphic symbols of a familiar language to ascertain their intended meaning

diphthong: a vowel sound produced when the tongue moves from one vowel sound toward another vowel in the same syllable; two vowel sounds that come together so fast that they are considered one syllable (ou, ow, oi/oy)

fluency: freedom from word-identification problems that might hinder comprehension in silent reading or the expression of ideas in oral reading; automaticity, the ability to produce words or larger language units in a limited time interval

homographs: words that are spelled alike but have different sounds and meanings (bow and arrow vs. bow of a ship)

homonyms: words which sound the same but have different spellings and meanings (bear, bare)

independent reading level: the readability or grade level of material that is easy for a student to read with few word-identification problems and high comprehension

instructional reading level: the reading ability or grade level of material that is challenging, but not frustrating for the student to read successfully with normal classroom instruction and support

orthographic system–The orthographic system deals with the form of letters and the spelling patterns within words, orthographic awareness is what you see. It requires visual perception.

pacing: setting one's own reading rate by using a pattern appropriate for the reading task

phonemes: a minimal sound unit of speech that distinguishes one word from another (lace, lake)

phonemic awareness: a way of teaching reading and spelling that stresses symbol sound relationships; the ability to associate letters and letter combinations with sound and blending them into syllables and words

phonics: a way of teaching reading and spelling that stresses symbol sound relationships; the ability to associate letters and letter combinations with sound and blending them into syllables and words

phonological system –is the sound of language. It is what you hear, phonological awareness means hearing the sounds in words. It is the realization that words are made up of sequences of sounds.

transitional spelling: the result of an attempt to spell a word whose spelling is not already known, based on a writer's knowledge of the spelling system and how it works

vowel digraph: two vowels pronounced in such a way that the letters together stand for one sound (/a/ in sleigh)

Chapter 19

CST MULTI—ELA SUBAREA

The **ELA** section tests your ability as an educator to guide your students through English Language Arts. This section includes understanding language, a familiarity of terminology in reading and writing education and also knowledge of children's book authors.

0001 Foundations of reading development

If the child is not exposed to language by a certain age, he/she will never fully develop language capabilities

Beginning reading approaches

- Bottom-up or code emphasis approach
- Top-down or meaning emphasis approach. Whole language, individualized reading programs.

Developmental reading approaches

- Basal reading core of most programs
- Phonics
- Linguistic approach
- Whole language
- Individualized Reading

0002 Strategies involved in reading comprehension

Hierarchy of the developmental stages of reading

- Word consciousness
- Language and conventions of print
- Functions of print
- Fluency

Use below for the essay part of the exam as well

Constructing meaning from the text:

- Word knowledge (lexical)
- Syntax and context
- Semantic knowledge
- Text organization

Characteristics of good readers

- Think about information they read, formulate questions.
- Attack unfamiliar words by using analogies to familiar words or by pronouncing them
- Before reading they establish a purpose for reading, choose reading strategy and make predictions about the text
- While reading, they confirm predictions, go back to check the text and make new predictions.

Terms You Should Know For Reading Instruction:

affix: A word element that is placed at the beginning (prefix), in the middle (infix), or at the end (suffix) of the root or word stem.

alliteration: The repetition of the same or similar sounds (usually consonants) that are close to one another (e.g. the timid, tiny tadpole).

alphabetic principle: The idea that letters represent sound and that printed letters can be turned into speech (and vice versa).

anecdotal records: An informal, written record (usually positive in tone), based on the observations of the teacher, of a student's progress and/or activities which occur throughout the day.

antonym: A word which is the opposite of another word. *Large* is the antonym of *small.*

balanced literacy: Generally, an approach to reading that incorporates both whole language and phonics instruction.

blending: Combining parts of words to form a word. For example, combining *pl* and *ate* to form *plate.*

book talk: When a teacher (or media specialist) gives a brief talk about a particular book to generate interest in the book.

choral reading: Sometimes referred to as unison reading. The whole class reads the same text aloud. Usually the teacher sets the pace. Choral reading helps with the ability to read sight words and builds fluency.

chunking: Reading by grouping portions of text into short, meaningful phrases.

cloze: A procedure whereby a word or words has/have been removed from a sentence and the student must fill in the blank using context clues (clues in the sentence).

consonant: a letter and a sound. Consonants are the letters of the alphabet except for the vowels *a, e, i, o, u* and sometimes *y* and *w.*

consonant blend: two or three consonants grouped together; each sound is retained (heard). For example: *st* and *scr.*

consonant digraph: two or more consonants grouped together in which the consonants produce one sound. For example: *sh* and *ch.*

consonant cluster: A group of consonants that appear together in a syllable without a vowel between them.

context clues: Bits of information from the text that, when combined with the reader's own knowledge, allow the reader to **"read between the lines,"** figure out the meaning of the text, or determine the meaning of unknown words in the text.

D.E.A.R: Drop Everything and Read. A time set aside during the school day in which everyone (teachers and students) drop everything and read.

decode: to analyze graphic symbols to determine their intended meaning.

duet reading: When a skilled reader and a weaker, less-skilled reader reads the same text aloud. The skilled reader may be a peer, older sibling, parent, or teacher. Duet reading builds confidence and fluency.

easy reader: A short book with appropriately short text. The illustrations amplify the text.

echo reading: When a skilled reader reads a portion of text (sometimes just a sentence) while the less-skilled reader "tracks." The less-skilled reader then imitates or "echoes" the skilled reader.

emergent reader: An emergent reader: has print awareness, reads in a left-to-right and top-to-bottom progression, uses some beginning and ending letter sounds, may tell the story from memory, may invent text, interprets/uses picture clues to help tell the story, is beginning to use high-frequency words.

environmental print: Print that is all around us: street signs, labels on cans or jars, handwritten notes, etc.

expository writing: Text that explains an event, concept, or idea using facts and examples.

fluency: The ability to read at an appropriate rate smoothly. (Also the ability to read expressively if reading aloud.)

fluent reader: A fluent reader: reads quickly, smoothly, and with expression; has a large store of sight words; automatically decodes unknown words, self-corrects.

genre: A type or category of literature marked by conventions of style, format, and/or content. Genres include: mystery, fantasy, epic poetry, etc.

grapheme: The smallest unit of a writing system. A grapheme may be one letter such as *t* or combination of letters such as *sh*. A grapheme represents one **phoneme.**

guided reading: A context wherein the teacher interacts with small groups of students as they read books that present a challenge. The teacher introduces reading strategies, tailoring the instruction to the needs of the students. When the students read, the teacher provides praise and encouragement as well as support when needed. Proponents of guided reading, Irene C. Fountas and Gay Su Pinell, have stated, "The ultimate goal of guided reading is to help children learn how to use independent reading strategies successfully."

homograph: Two words that have the same spelling but different meanings and/or origins and may differ in pronunciation. Example: "the *bow* of a ship" and "a hair *bow*"

homonym: A word that has the same spelling or pronunciation as another but different meanings and/or origins. See homograph and homophone.

homophone: Two words that have the same pronunciation but differ in meaning or spelling or both. Example: pause and paws

idiom: a phrase or expression that is (usually) not taken literally. For example, "Don't let the cat out of the bag" means to not tell something one knows, to keep silent.

independent reading: Students self select books to read. A student's "independent reading level" is the level at which the student can read with 96-100% accuracy.

language experience approach: Also referred to as LEA. An approach to literacy instruction in which students orally dictate texts to a teacher (or scribe). The text is then read aloud by the teacher as the students read along silently. Students are then encouraged to read and re-read the text, thus building fluency. The experiences that serve as stimuli/sources for the dictated text can vary from literature discussions to field trips. Generally, the approach involves: a shared experience, discussion, oral dictation, reading, and re-reading. After the shared experience, the scribe helps the student write about the experience. The approach works not only with beginning readers, but non-native speakers of English, and adult learners as well. LEA is not a new approach; It has been studied and used for decades.

learning log: A document wherein students write entries (usually short and ungraded) which reflect upon a lesson, activity, event, discussion, presentation, or experiment.

leveled text: Books are "leveled" (i.e. placed in a certain category) based on the criteria of the person or entity leveling the books. Irene C. Fountas and Gay Su Pinnell, the developers of Guided Reading, advocate these stages: Emergent Readers (Levels A-E); Early Readers (Levels F-J); Early Fluent Readers (Levels K-P); and Fluent Readers (Levels Q-W). Individual titles of books are then given a "level" based upon certain criteria. The Lexile Framework is another such tool. Lexile measures reader ability and text difficulty by the same standard. The leveling of texts allows teachers to match books with an individual student's reading ability.

literacy: The ability to read, write, communicate, and comprehend.

literacy centers: Stations or areas where literacy activities are set up for use. Centers may also be portable wherein the student takes the "center" to his or her desk. Examples of literacy centers: Reading the Room (a small area where students may obtain a flyswatter, pointer, large glasses, etc. that they can use to "read" the room as them walk around). Writing Centers which have available various types of paper, writing utensils, stamps, etc. For younger children the Writing Center may contain materials which they can use to form letters or words such play dough, finger paint, a flat piece of velvet, etc.

literature circles: Student-led book discussion groups. Students choose their own reading material and meet in small, temporary groups with other students who are reading the same book. The teacher acts a facilitator. Literature Circles by Harvey Daniels (Stenhouse Publishers) is considered by many to be the definitive guide on the subject.

main idea: The point the author is making about a topic. Topic and main idea are not the same.

metaphor: A figure of speech in which two things are compared by saying one thing *is* another.

modeled reading: Wherein the teacher reads aloud a book which is above the students' reading level. Students may or may not have a copy of the text with which to follow along. The purpose of modeled reading is to demonstrate a skill or ability such as: fluency, fix-up strategy, think aloud.

morpheme: the smallest unit of meaning in oral and written language.

narrative writing: Generally, writing about an event in a personal way.

onset: The initial consonant sound (or sounds) that come before the vowel in a syllable. For example, the onset of *cat* is *c*. (The remainder of the word–*at*–is called a rime.)

orthography: the written letters or symbols of a language.

paired reading: see *duet reading* above

pattern books: Also referred to as predictable books. Books which use repetitive language and/or scenes, sequences, episodes. Predictable books allow early readers to predict what the sentences are going to say, thereby increasing enjoyment and helping to build vocabulary.

phoneme: The smallest unit of speech that affects the meaning of a word. A sound unit. The *c* in cat and the *m* in mat are phonemes.

phonemic awareness: The awareness of sounds in spoken words. A subset of phonological awareness. Phonemic awareness and phonics are not the same. Phonemic awareness is the ability to orally hear, identify, and manipulate individual sounds or segments of sound in words. Research has identified phonemic awareness as an essential and necessary ability if the child is become a good reader.

phonics: A method of teaching reading that focuses on letter-sound relationships.

phonogram: Also referred to as *rime* or *word family*. All the sounds (after the onset) from the vowel to the end of the word.

predictable books: Also referred to as pattern books. Books which use repetitive language and/or scenes, sequences, episodes. Predictable books allow early readers to predict what the sentences are going to say, thereby increasing enjoyment and helping to build vocabulary.

prefix: An affix that is added to the front of a word and changes its meaning. For example: *un* being placed in front of the word *developed.*

print conventions: The rules of print. For example: In the West one reads from left to right and moves from the top to the bottom of the page. Research shows that three of the most important and fundamental concepts students need to learn to become readers are: knowledge of the alphabet, phonemic awareness, and conventions of print.

prior knowledge: Knowledge which the reader has prior to engaging in the lesson or reading. Sometimes referred to as schema. It is important to activate prior knowledge before the lesson or reading. This allows students to connect what they are learning/reading with what they already know. Additionally, a discussion of prior knowledge alerts the teacher to gaps in the students' knowledge and/or misconceptions the students have.

r controlled vowel: When a vowel is followed by the letter *r* and this causes the vowel sound to be altered. For example: *her.*

reading wars: A "war" waged primarily in the 1980s and 1990s over the best way to teach reading. On one side: the proponents of phonics, on the other the proponents of whole language. Today, the general consensus among researchers and reading specialists is a balanced approach. A list of online resources concerning the debate may be found <u>here.</u>

reader's workshop: In a reader's workshop the teacher begins by presenting a mini-lesson on a reading skill or concept. Students are then given uninterrupted time to read their various texts. Afterward students respond to what they have read in a reader response journal or reading log. Many reading workshops also include time for sharing. Many teachers first became familiar with reading workshops through Nancy Atwell's classic book *In the Middle* published in the late 1980s . The latest edition of the book is titled <u>In the Middle : New Understanding About Writing, Reading, and Learning</u> (Boynton-Cook/Heinemann). Another extremely popular book which discusses the reader's workshop is *<u>Mosaic of Thought: Teaching Comprehension in a Reader's Workshop</u>* by Ellin Oliver Keene and Susan Zimmerman (Heinemann).

reading in the content areas: Concerns the ability to read, write, speak about (as well as listen to) subject matter across the curriculum. The pioneers on this topic are Richard Vacca and Jo Anne Vacca who wrote *<u>Content Area Reading: Literacy and Learning Across the Curriculum</u>* (Pearson/Allyn & Bacon).

reading response logs: A notebook or binder wherein students can respond to their reading. Reading response logs may take many forms. Teachers may wish to assign a prompt (or selection of prompts) which the students will then write about. Or, they can be used to document: reflections of the student, feelings about the reading, details of the text which interested the students, etc.

rime: Also referred to *word family*. All the sounds (after the onset) from the vowel to the end of the word. For example the rime in the word *cat* is *at*. (The onset is *c*.)

running records: In reading, a teacher records the child's reading behavior as he or she reads a book. The teacher may note errors, self-corrections, substitutions, and so forth. Also known as reading assessments. Teachers generally use a standard set of symbols for recording what the reader does while reading.

schwa: the sound "uh." For example, the vowel sound heard at the beginning of the word *alone*. The schwa is represented by the symbol /a/ and any of the vowel letters (lett*u*ce).

semantics: the branch of linguistics which studies meaning in language.

shared reading: An activity in which the teacher reads a story while the students look at the text being read and follow along. During this time the teacher may introduce print conventions, teach vocabulary, introduce a reading skill, encourage predictions, and more. The shared reading model was developed by Don Holdaway in 1979.

sight word: Words that good readers instantly recognize without having to decode them. Sight words are usually "high-frequency" words.

silent, sustained reading: A period of time wherein students read silently from a book or other text of their choice.

suffix: A group of letters added to the end of a word to form a new word. For example: when *ful* is added to the word *help*, a new word is formed: *helpful*.

syllable: a unit of sound or group of letters made up of a vowel sound or a vowel consonant combination. Syllables contain only one vowel.

synonym: A word that has the same meaning as another word. For example: *big* and *large* are synonyms.

syntax: the word order pattern in sentences, phrases, etc.

synthesize: The process of combining two separate elements into one new element.

topic: What the text is about. The topic is not the same as the main idea.

vowel: a letter and a sound. The vowels in the alphabet are represented by the letters *a, e, i, o, u* and sometimes *y* and *w*.

vowel digraph: a group of two vowels in which only one sound is heard. For example: he*i*ght.

vowel diphthong: the blending of two vowel sounds. For example: b*oi*l. Also referred to as a vowel blend.

Whole Language Approach: A holistic philosophy of reading instruction which gained momentum during the 1970s, '80s, and early '90s. Emphasizes the use of authentic text, reading for meaning, the integration of all language skills (reading, writing, speaking, and listening), and context.

word analysis: The identification and/or decoding or a word the reader does not immediately recognize.

word families: Also known as phonograms, word families are groups of words that have a common pattern. For example, the *an* word family contains the words *fan, pan, ran, plan, man*, and so on.

word segmentation: The ability to break words into individual syllables.

word wall: An area of the classroom (such as a bulletin board) on which a collection of words are displayed. (Personal word walls can be made using file folders.)

(Source: The Education Oasis)

Classroom Instruction Questions:

My best advice for this section would be to read the section of this book devoted to the ATS-W. In that part there is a chapter devoted to the Constructivist Approach that is used in Education in NY State. Unfortunately the rules of this approach are not often followed by working educators. Therefore many teachers will repeatedly fail this section because they answer the questions based on what they are doing in the classroom rather than the actual rule of the Department of Education. I will not repeat that information here. However I will repeat the Trap Words to Avoid. If you see any of these words in potential answers, eliminate it. It is the wrong answer.

Trap Words to Avoid:

Separate
Isolate
Make a special assignment
Have a co teacher work
separately
Special seating arrangements
So as not to embarrass
Pair, partner, buddy up
Group according to academic
ability
Peer friendships
Memorize
Commit to memory
Recite
Rote Learning
Fill out a handout or
worksheet
Read a book, hand out etc.
(read should be followed by
discuss)

Lecture
Teacher assigned
Teacher chosen
Teacher centered
Teach
Assign
"takes too much time'
"try harder"
Change
Ignore
Argue
Refuse
General and inclusive
Give in
Give up
Acquiesce
Compliance

Here are some examples of questions I have seen that use these words to trap you into the wrong answer.

Books You Should Know:

Many times on the exam there will be questions that ask you the name of the author of a famous children's book. If you don't know the answer then these questions should be approached as an elimination question. You simply eliminate the wrong answers until you are left with the correct one. In order to do this you should familiarize yourself with famous children's book writers and their styles.

Here is a list of one hundred books selected by the National Education Association as great reading for children and young people.

At the end of this list I will examine the writing style of some of the authors on this list. Sometimes the questions on the exam also ask you what kind of book an author is famous for writing.

Books for All Ages

The Giving Tree by Shel Silverstein
Where the Sidewalk Ends: the Poems and Drawing of Shel Silverstein by Shel Silverstein
Little Women by Louisa May Alcott
The Wizard of Oz by L. Frank Baum
Heidi by Johanna Spyri

Books for Preschoolers
The Very Hungry Caterpillar by Eric Carle
Goodnight Moon by Margaret Wise Brown
Brown Bear, Brown Bear, What do you see? by Bill Martin, Jr.
The Rainbow Fish by Marcus Pfister
Corduroy by Don Freeman
The Snowy Day by Ezra Jack Keats
The Runaway Bunny by Margaret Wise
Guess How Much I Love You by Sam McBratney

Books for Children Ages 4-8 –
The Polar Express by Chris Van Allsburg
Green Eggs and Ham by Dr. Seuss
The Cat in the Hat by Dr. Seuss
Where the Wild Things Are by Maurice Sendak
Love You Forever by Robert N. Munsch
Alexander and the Terrible, Horrible, No Good, Very Bad Day by Judith Viorst
The Mitten by Jan Brett
Stellaluna by Janell Cannon
Oh, The Places You'll Go by Dr. Seuss
Strega Nona by Tomie De Paola

The Velveteen Rabbit by Margery Williams
How the Grinch Stole Christmas by Dr. Seuss
The True Story of the Three Little Pigs by Jon Scieszka
Chicka Chicka Boom Boom by John Archambault
The Complete Tales of Winnie the Pooh by A. A. Milne
If You Give a Mouse a Cookie by Laura Joffe Numeroff
The Lorax by Dr. Seuss
Amazing Grace by Mary Hoffman
Jumanji by Chris Van Allsburg
Math Curse by Jon Scieszka
Are You My Mother? by Philip D. Eastman
The Napping House by Audrey Wood
Sylvester and the Magic Pebble by William Steig
The Tale of Peter Rabbit by Beatrix Potter
Horton Hatches the Egg by Dr. Seuss
Basil of Baker Street by Eve Titus
The Little Engine That Could by Watty Piper
Curious George by Hans Augusto Rey
Wilfrid Gordon McDonald Partridge by Mem Fox
Arthur series by Marc Tolon Brown
Lilly's Purple Plastic Purse by Kevin Henkes
The Little House by Virginia Lee Burton
Amelia Bedelia by Peggy Parish
The Art Lesson by Tomie De Paola
Caps for Sale by Esphyr Slobodkina
Clifford, the Big Red Dog by Norman Bridwell
The Paper Bag Princess by Robert N. Munsch

Books for Children Ages 9-12
Charlotte's Web by E. B. White
Hatchet by Gary Paulsen
The Lion, the Witch, and the Wardrobe by C. S. Lewis
Bridge to Terabithia by Katherine Paterson
Charlie and the Chocolate Factory by Roald Dahl
A Wrinkle in Time by Madeleine L'Engle
Shiloh by Phyllis Reynolds Naylor
Little House on the Prarie by Laura Ingalls Wilder
The Secret Garden by Frances Hodgson Burnett

The Boxcar Children by Gertrude Chandler Warner
Sarah, Plain and Tall by Patricia MacLachlan
The Indian in the Cupboard by Lynne Reid Banks
Island of the Blue Dolphins by Scott O'Dell
Maniac Magee by Jerry Spinelli
The BFG by Roald Dahl
The Giver by Lois Lowry
James and the Giant Peach: A Children's Story by Roald Dahl
Little House in the Big Woods by Laura Ingalls Wilder
Roll of Thunder, Hear My Cry by Mildred D. Taylor
Stone Fox by John Reynolds Gardiner
Number the Stars by Lois Lowry
Mrs. Frisby and the Rats of Nimh by Robert C. O'Brien
The Best Christmas Pageant Ever by Barbara Robinson
Matilda by Roald Dahl
Tales of a Fourth Grade Nothing by Judy Blume
Ramona Quimby, Age 8 by Beverly Cleary
The Trumpet of the Swan by E. B. White
The Chronicles of Narnia by C. S. Lewis
The Phantom Tollbooth by Norton Juster
Tuck Everlasting by Natalie Babbitt
Anne of Green Gables by Lucy Maud Montgomery
The Great Gilly Hopkins by Katherine Paterson
Little House books by Laura Ingalls Wilder
Sideways Stories from Wayside School by Louis Sachar
Harriet the Spy by Louise Fitzhugh
A Light in the Attic by Shel Silverstein
Mr. Popper's Penguins by Richard Atwater
My Father's Dragon by Ruth Stiles Gannett
Stuart Little by E. B. White
Walk Two Moons by Sharon Creech
The Witch of Blackbird Pond by Elizabeth George Speare
The Watsons Go to Birmingham-1963 by Christopher Paul Curtis

Books for Young Adults –
Where the Red Fern Grows by Wilson Rawls
The Hobbit by J. R. R. Tolkien
Summer of the Monkeys by Wilson Rawls

The Cay by Theodore Taylor
The Sign of the Beaver by Elizabeth George Speare

Authors known for style or topic:

Most have won awards for writing:

Hans Christian Andersen: is a Danish author, wrote works in various genres, but he is best known for his fairy tales, which have been translated into more than 80 languages. Tales such as "The Ugly Duckling," "The Emperor's New Clothes," "The Snow Queen," and "The Little Mermaid" are considered classics and continue to be appreciated by readers of all ages.

Eric Carle is a children's book author and illustrator who is most famous for his book *The Very Hungry Caterpillar*. His art is distinctive and instantly recognizable. His art work is created in collage technique, using hand-painted papers, which he cuts and layers to form bright and colorful images. Many of his books have an added dimension—die-cut pages, twinkling lights as in *The Very Lonely Firefly*, even the lifelike sound of a cricket's song as in *The Very Quiet Cricket*.

Donald Crews: is an African American writer and illustrator of several well-known children's picture books. He won the Caldecott Honor twice. Common subjects of his include modern technology (especially travel vehicles), and childhood memories. His stories often include few humans. His award winning books include Freight Train and Trucks. He has also written books such as School Bus, Big Mama's and Inside Freight Train.

Roald Dahl: Roald Dahl is a European author who writes books about children in unusual circumstances. Usually they are unhappy children who find a sense of "escape" through an extraordinary end. Dahl's books are often made into movies. Some examples are *Charlie and the Chocolate Factory, Matilda, James and the Giant Peach,* and *The Witches.*

Tomie dePaola: is an American author and illustrator of over 200 children's books. His style is a combination of folks style picture books . Many of his books feature illustrations of a little boy often in the kitchen with his grandmother. Some of his books include: *The Art Lesson, Tommy's Bread, 26 Fairmount Avenue, Jamie O'Rourke and the Big Potato: An Irish Folktale, The Legend of the Bluebonnet: An Old Tale of Texas* and, *Strega Nona.*

Paul Goble: is an award winning author and illustrator of children's books, mostly Native American stories. Goble has received a number of honors for his books including the prestigious Caldecott Medal. *Star Boy, Hau Kola: Hello Friend, Mystic Horse, and Iktomi and the Boulder.* He has several books about the character Iktomi a Native American boy.

Ezra Jack Keats (born Jacob Ezra Katz), Caldecott-winning author of *The Snowy Day,* was one of the most important children's literature authors and illustrators of the 20th Century. Keats is best known for introducing multiculturalism into mainstream American children's literature. He was one of the first children's book authors use an urban setting for his stories and he developed the use of collage as a medium for illustration.

C.S Lewis: The books he is most famous for writing are included in the seven part series of Narnia: *The Chronicles of Narnia* is a series of seven fantasy novels for children written by C. S. Lewis. It is considered a classic of children's literature.

In addition to numerous traditional Christian themes, the series borrows characters and ideas from Greek and Roman mythology, as well as from traditional British and Irish fairy tales. *The Chronicles of Narnia* presents the adventures of children who play central roles in the unfolding history of the fictional realm of Narnia, a place where animals talk, magic is common, and good battles evil. Each of the books (with the exception of *The Horse and His Boy)* features as its protagonists children from our world who are magically transported to Narnia, where they are called upon by the lion Aslan to help Narnia and restore the throne to the rightful line. The most famous of these books is called *The Lion, the Witch and the Wardrobe.*

Pat Mora: is a Hispanic author known primarily for her poetry and children's books. She is also well known for her bilingual books. Some of her famous works include: *Abuelos, Agua, Agua, Agua, This Big Sky, Gracias/Thanks, Confetti: Poems for Children,Confeti: Poemas para niños (Spanish edition), Delicious Hullabaloo: Pachanga deliciosa (bilingual)* and *The Desert Is My Mother/El desierto es mi madre(bilingual)*

Maurice Bernard Sendak: is an American writer and illustrator of children's literature. Sendak gained international acclaim after writing and illustrating *Where the Wild Things Are,* although the book's depictions of fanged monsters concerned some parents when it was first released, as his characters were somewhat grotesque in appearance. Sendak's seeming attraction to the forbidden or nightmarish aspects of children's fantasy have made him a subject of controversy. The monsters in the book were actually based on relatives who would come to weekly dinners. He also was a source of controversy for his book *In the Night Kitchen* which depicted nudity on a little boy dreaming of being small enough to wander through the kitchen counters and cabinets. His other famous books include books for very young children:

The Nutshell Library

- *Alligators All Around (An Alphabet)*
- *Chicken Soup with Rice (A Book of Months)*
- *One Was Johnny (A Counting Book)*
- *Pierre (A Cautionary Tale)*

Dr Seuss: (real name: Theodor Geisel) Dr. Seuss was a children's book writer, illustrator and poet. Almost all of his books use rhyme and rhythm and phonics sounds in order to teach reading. Dr. Seuss will often make up imaginative words to keep the rhyme and pace flowing. He regularly uses made up creatures in his stories like: *How the Grinch Stole Christmas, Sneetches,* and *The Lorax.* He is famous for these and other books like *The Cat in the Hat* and *Horton Hears a Who* etc. He also uses his own illustrations in his books.

Shel Silverstein: was famous for children's poetry book collections. The most famous of his works include *The Giving Tree, Where the Sidewalk Ends, A Light in the Attic,* and *Falling Up.*

Laura Elizabeth Ingalls Wilder was an American author who wrote the *Little House* series of books based on her childhood in a pioneer family. The most famous of her books is *The Little House on the Prairie.*

(Source NYSTCE Preparation Guides and Wikipedia)

Chapter 20

RESOURCES FOR ADDITIONAL STUDY

ATS-W

NYSTCE ATS-W Practice Test Links\
Elementary Assessment of Teaching Skills–Written (090)
Secondary Assessment of Teaching Skills–Written (091)

Constructivist Theory
http://en.wikipedia.org/wiki/Constructivism_(learning_theory)

Piaget's Theory of Cognitive Development
http://en.wikipedia.org/wiki/Theory_of_cognitive_development

Maslow
http://en.wikipedia.org/wiki/Abraham_Maslow#Hierarchy_of_needs

Practice Essay Links
http://www.brooklyn.liu.edu/bbut07/writingc/wc_atsw_decode.html
http://www.brooklyn.liu.edu/bbut07/writingc/wc_atsw_develop.html
http://www.brooklyn.liu.edu/bbut07/writingc/wc_atsw_sample.html

Stages of Intellectual Development In Children and Teenagers
http://www.childdevelopmentinfo.com/development/piaget.shtml

CST Students with Disabilities

Writing Clinical Documents
http://student.brooklynedu.org/WritingClinicalDocuments.pdf

Content Specialty Test (CST)–Students with Disabilities
http://premdisplay.com/touro/tourowebed/cstdisability.htm

MY CHILD'S SPECIAL NEEDS A Guide to the Individualized
Education Program
http://www.ed.gov/parents/needs/speced/iepguide/index.html

Series on Highly Effective Practices/Transitions
http://education.odu.edu/esse/research/series/transitions.shtml

Medina House School Assessment–Recording–Reporting
http://www.medinahouseschool.co.uk/uploads/Assessment%20
Recording%20and%20Reporting%20Policy.pdf

Teaching the Self-Advocacy Strategy
http://www.nsttac.org/pdf/ebps/self_advocacy.pdf

Stages of Intellectual Development In Children and Teenagers
http://www.childdevelopmentinfo.com/development/piaget.shtml

Types of Disabilities
http://web.jhu.edu/disabilities/faculty/types_of_disabilities/index.
html

CST Multi Subject

Memorizing For the Mathematics portion of your NYSTCE Multi-Subject
CST test
http://www.teachingsolutions.org/nystce31.html

Building A Powerful Reading Program: From Research to Practice
http://www.csus.edu/ier/reading.html

Stages of Intellectual Development In Children and Teenagers
http://www.childdevelopmentinfo.com/development/piaget.shtml

Fellows' Guide to the Multi-subject CST
http://www.brooklynedu.org/OnlineDocs/fellowsguidetomulti-subjectcst.html

Meta-fiction
http://en.wikipedia.org/wiki/Metafiction

Online Grammar Quizzes
http://www.syntaxis.com/index.php/grammar_quiz/grammar_quiz/

It Pays to Enrich Your Word Power
http://mercury.tvu.ac.uk/~alan/word_power/choose.php

Online Math Quizzes
http://www.math.com/students/practice.html

Art links
http://en.wikipedia.org/wiki/Pop_art
http://en.wikipedia.org/wiki/Impressionism
http://en.wikipedia.org/wiki/Renaissance_art

American History Timelines
http://www.animatedatlas.com/timeline.html
http://www.cloudnet.com/~edrbsass/educationhistorytimeline.html

Some important history
http://en.wikipedia.org/wiki/The_Civil_Rights_Movement
http://www.historyplace.com/worldwar2/timeline/ww2time.htm

1968 this is a 6 part video series that goes over one year in the 60's that gives a good overview of American History in that Era. Please note that it is ONLY about 1968, therefore it doesn't include the March on Washington.

http://www.youtube.com/watch?v=6vVZP2T60wI
http://www.youtube.com/watch?v=hynKUzZtDuw&feature=fvw
http://www.youtube.com/watch?v=hynKUzZtDuw&feature=fvw
http://www.youtube.com/watch?v=VyCYmqIrZdo&feature=related
http://www.youtube.com/watch?v=0l4n5uw_GFM&feature=related
http://www.youtube.com/watch?v=3tOMk5IpygA&feature=related

This is a documentary of the Native American plight in the US.
http://www.youtube.com/watch?v=jOfEAbNiKFM
http://www.youtube.com/watch?v=BGuNpPt_tfw&NR=1
http://www.youtube.com/watch?v=Rw7vKerABME

More about the Removal
http://www.youtube.com/watch?v=I3gNzfMobNI
http://www.youtube.com/watch?v=bWCl9YfbKa4&feature=related
http://www.youtube.com/watch?v=Iycym3JonJk&NR=1

CPSIA information can be obtained at www.ICGtesting.com
Printed in the USA
BVOW07s1239290813

329763BV00002B/564/P

9 781456 850333